Date With Destiny

The Kenza Gumbs Story

Kenza Gumbs

FOREWORD BY
Kwesi Gumbs

Copyright © 2018 by Kenza Gumbs
https://www.datewithdestinytkgs.com
Kenza Gumbs, P.O. Box 1229, Grayson, GA 30017

All rights reserved. In accordance with the U.S. Copyright Act of 1976, the scanning, uploading, and electronic sharing of any part of this book without the permission of the publisher is unlawful piracy and theft of the author's intellectual property. If you would like to use material from the book, prior written permission must be obtained by contacting the publisher at info@entegritypublishing.com.
Thank you for your support of the author's rights.

Entegrity Choice Publishing
PO Box 453
Powder Springs, GA 30127
info@entegritypublishing.com
www.entegritypublishing.com
770.727.6517

Printed in the United States of America

The views expressed in this work are solely those of the author and do not necessarily reflect the views of the publisher, and the publisher hereby disclaims any responsibility for them.

The publisher is not responsible for websites (or their content) that are not owned by the publisher.

Library of Congress Cataloging-in-Publication Data
ISBN 978-1-7325767-1-1
Library of Congress 2018951887

Acknowledgements

To my awesome King Potentate, Jesus Christ, be all the glory, honor, and praise. It is because of You, I can share this testimony.

A big thank you to all of my precious "Familia" for the awesome outpouring of love and abundant support in sharing this testimony.

To Lucille Gumbs aka Mom, for your much-needed pep talks and Charles Gumbs aka Grand, for your behind - the- scenes care and encouragement – thank you.

I wholeheartedly thank my Mother dearest, Claudette Thomas for your labor of love through it all. Will be forever grateful.

I'm grateful to my best friend and confidant, Kendra Roach aka Twinny. You were a source of strength despite your days of having your own challenges with school. Love yah.

Expression of thanks to my big Sister Anuska "Nuxie" Callwood and Gertrude "Auntie Trudy" Saunders for the exceptional editing assistance. I

Acknowledgements

had no idea you both are so creative. The time came for this incredible creative measure to be released in this testimony, and for that I am forever grateful.

I acknowledge my awesome brother, Pastor Kwesi Gumbs aka "Big Bro" for your guidance along the way. Your constructive criticism pushed me forward in the best way ever. Forever grateful.

I send out a big thank you to my Sister in Law Dr. Wanda Gumbs for your love, support and care through it all. Bountiful blessings be upon you.

I appreciate my family and friends who did not have a problem with me sharing the pictures in this testimony.

I am indebted to my Cornerstone family for the much-needed prayers and support.

Lastly, I am thankful to my readers for their interest in this awesome testimony, which, I am one hundred percent sure, will encourage you during your appointed "date with destiny". King Jesus, whom we serve, is no respecter of persons. Rest assured that the same way He miraculously helped me, He will do the same or even greater for you. Just humble yourself and ask Him!

Contents

Acknowledgements 3
Foreword 7
Introduction 9
Chapter 1
    The Suddenly 11
Chapter 2
    Good Always Comes Out Of Bad 23
Chapter 3
    Delayed But Not Denied 29
Chapter 4
    The Number of Completion 39
Chapter 5
    Set Times And Seasons For Everything ... 49
Chapter 6
    Tell The Truth And Shame The Devil 59
Chapter 7
    Transformation Starts in the Mind
    and Heart 69
Chapter 8
    All Things Work Together For Good 77

Chapter 9
    Mercy Always Triumphs Over Judgment . 89
Chapter 10
    Weeping May Endure For The Night BUT Joy Is Coming 99
Chapter 11
    Waiting On The Lord Is Always Best. . . . 111
References. 123

Foreword

Life is a wonderful gift, yet there are seasons of testing in our lives, when we struggle to maintain a healthy appreciation for the gift of life. Trials, challenges, and disappointments may seem to squeeze all the life out of us, yet in moments of utter hopelessness, the indomitable persistence of the human spirit rises within us and thrives. Kenza's story is indicative of this experience and is a testament of how fragile life can be. In a moment, all that we know to be normal can be radically changed, leaving us isolated, confused, and even angry.

In moments like these, we need to draw strength from someone stronger, wiser, and more experienced; Jesus Christ is the only suitable choice. He brings hope to hopeless situations and reveals His unseen hand working in the background, making all things work for our good. My desire for those reading this story is that we will begin to see trials as opportunities to draw closer to God and reasons to strengthen our desire for Him.

We often forget the promise Jesus made when

Foreword

He said, "In this world you will have trouble, but be of good cheer because I have overcome the world." So, take heart, my friend. You are not alone! He is with you, fighting for you, protecting you, and bringing you to that expected end. Your role is to press on and see what the end will be when you have your date with destiny!

Kwesi Gumbs, Campus Pastor
Fresh Anointing House of Worship
Atlanta, GA

Introduction

We know that there is nothing new under the sun: *"Whatever is has already been, and what will be has been before." Ecclesiastes 3:15 (NIV)*

This book is to encourage and remind you that everything happens in our lives at designated times and, better yet, for appointed purposes established before the foundation of this world. Perhaps you are currently going through a divorce, or you are in the midst of death, that is the death of a spouse, parent, sibling, or child, or the loss of a job that you thought was secure.

These times spoken of are the appointed times of our lives known as our "Date with Destiny" and, depending on one's spiritual state of existence at the appointed time of one's date, will determine whether we will mount up with wings like eagles or succumb to the pressures of the circumstance with depression, addictions, or, in worse cases, suicide.

My prayer for each one reading the words of this testimony is that the eyes of your understanding will be enlightened and transformed into a new

Introduction

depth of awareness for your life in Jesus' name. You will be thankful to God, knowing with all your heart that "all things," including this awesome date with destiny, are working together for your good because you are called according to His intended purpose.

Be blessed and encouraged!
Kenza Gumbs

1
The Suddenly

My alarm clock woke me up at 6:00 am Sunday morning on March 15, 2015. I turned off my alarm and reached for my morning devotion, pondered and meditated on it, then gently prayed, asking the Lord for His will to be done in my space today. I asked Him to let all I did and said be a reflection of Him. I ended my prayer by putting the enemy of my soul under my feet where he belongs.

I got up and organized myself by picking out an outfit that I would wear for an Ordination service for my dear friend scheduled for later that day. She and I met in a local seminary in Atlanta. Neither of us graduated from that seminary, but we maintained a genuine friendship and supported each other despite.

I prepared myself and stayed focused, so I could be out of the house by 8:55 a.m. and be on time to teach Sunday school. You see I am an ordained minister of the gospel of Jesus Christ, Sunday school teacher, Vacation Bible School instructor, Christian counselor, Board member, and pretty much an all-round worker for the Lord. I arrived at 9:20 a.m., gathered my purse and other belongings, and took them downstairs to one of the church offices. Sunday school went well as planned. We then transitioned into the morning service. It is always refreshing to be together with like minds and, as always, the Word of God does exactly what it is supposed to do.

Psalm 19:7 - *"The law of the Lord is perfect converting or reviving the soul; the testimony of the Lord is sure, making wise the simple."*

It is truly awesome being in the presence of the Lord, where there is fullness of joy and this joy cannot be taken away from us unless we make the choice to give it away.

After fellowship had ended, my beloved cousins and I went to our local buffet spot and enjoyed the food and family time. After my incredible crawfish special, we parted ways. I decided to make a stop at CVS pharmacy on the way home to pick out a wonderful card filled with encouraging words, coupled with a gift card, as my token of congratulations to a dear lady.

I finally arrived home and decided to catch

The Suddenly

an hour nap. My alarm was set for 2:45 p.m., and it did what it normally does, which was to wake me up, of course. Wanting at least ten more minutes of sleep, I decided against it and pushed myself to get up.

I refreshed my make-up, put my outfit on that I picked out earlier, and jumped into my car. While getting my mind together to go to my destination, I punched into the GPS the location of the intended address, which said it took forty minutes to arrive. I left home with every intention to be present and in full support of my dear friend on this awesome spiritual promotion. I took the shortest route I knew to get to Interstate 20. It is unclear, however, what happened entirely, but it happened.

I met my "Date with Destiny" on March 15, 2015, at 3:39 p.m. on Turner Hill Road and Covington Highway with a heavy-duty freight train. I do not remember anything at all, but from the police report to the newspaper clippings, TV reports, and one witness who shared their recollection of the event, this is what I have concluded.

Shortly after I rolled onto the train tracks, the crossing arms came down, and I ended up getting stuck. I tried to move forward, then backward, but could not and was hit on the passenger's side of my vehicle by the freight train, carrying two locomotives and thirty-eight rail cars. My car was dragged and propelled about one thousand feet in circular motion and ended up hitting another vehicle on the adjacent side of the tracks.

Let me pause here for a moment to encourage my readers. For those of you who do not know Christ as Savior, let me encourage you to accept Him before you encounter your "date with destiny" or your appointment with death. Hebrews 9:27 tells us, *"It is appointed unto man once to die, but after this the judgment."* One day we will all meet our Savior and must give an account of what we have done with the time He granted us here on earth. Jesus died on the cross to save us from our sins.

You may say that you are not a sinful or bad person, or that God is a loving God, and He will not punish you or send you to hell. But the Word of God says in Romans 3:23 (NIV), *"For all have sinned and fallen short of the glory of God."* From the moment we are born into this world, we become sinful. Sin entered the world through the first man named Adam and has spread to all his offspring.

Romans 5:18-19 - "Through one man's trespass or sins, judgment came to all men, for by one man's disobedience all were made sinners."

We are all born with a ready-made death warrant, which is our sin nature, because we have inherited this sin nature from Adam. We are already born spiritually dead or separated from God and die physically. *"For as in Adam all die, so in Christ all will be made alive."* 1 Corinthians 15:22 (NIV)

Death came through Adam, and the resurrection can only come to mankind by believing in Jesus Christ. What is God's solution to this sin nature? The Bible tells us that God gave us the way back into a relationship with Him, to be born again spiritually.

In John 3:3-7 (NIV), Jesus said to Nicodemus, *"Very truly I tell you, no one can see the kingdom of God unless he is born again." "How can someone be born when he is old?" Nicodemus asked. "Surely he cannot enter a second time into his mother's womb to be born!" Jesus answered, "Very truly I tell you, no one can enter the kingdom of God unless he is born of water and the Spirit. Flesh gives birth to flesh, but the Spirit gives birth to spirit. You should not be surprised at my saying, 'You must be born again.'*

God gave us His son and the gospel to believe in to be restored. Romans 10:10 (NKJV) - *"For with the heart one believes unto righteousness, and with the mouth confession is made unto salvation."* To be saved, one must believe not only in their mind but in their spirit also, which is their innermost being.

If you are willing to accept Him right now, you can ask Jesus to save you. If you want to be saved right now, repeat this prayer right where you are, believing in your heart and confessing with your mouth. Pray these words out loud:

"Lord Jesus, I have kept You out of my life for way too long. I know that I am a sinner and that I cannot save myself. I hear You knocking on the door of my heart. No longer will I choose to keep the door to my heart closed, but in faith, I believe in and receive Your gift of salvation. I am ready to trust You as my Lord and Savior. Thank You, Lord Jesus, for coming to earth. I believe You are the Son of God Who died on the cross for my sins and rose from the dead on the third day. Thank You for bearing my sins and giving me the gift of eternal life. I believe Your words are true. Come into my heart, Lord Jesus, and be my Savior now and forever." Amen.

For those of you who in the past have accepted Jesus as your Savior but have strayed away, I am admonishing you to return to your first love. There is nothing in this world that can satisfy you like the Lord. God still cares about you, and He has a plan that still includes you. Jeremiah 29: 11-14 (ESV) says: *"For I know the plans I have for you, declares the Lord, plans for welfare and not for evil, to give you a future and a hope. Then you will call upon Me and come and pray to Me, and I will hear you. You will seek Me and find Me, when you seek Me with all your heart. I will be found by you, declares the Lord, and I will restore your fortunes and gather you from all the nations and all the places where I have driven you, declares the Lord, and I will bring you back to the place from which I sent you into exile."*

I encourage you today to stop where you are and reach out to God before your date with destiny. You see, God punishes the sinner through divine discipline because He hates sin. Since the foundation of this world, God has established certain laws and principles, for example, the law of gravity. He also established colors, shapes, textures, and sound. In the same way, God has also given us countless spiritual principles that we can learn in the Bible and live by them.

God's principles are practical and life-transforming for those of us who choose to learn, know, and follow them, for example, the law of sowing and reaping. Whatever you sow you shall reap. It is not His will to punish anyone, nor does He want to suppress His Spirit from anyone. But His word does not lie.

God has natural and moral laws in place that punish sin directly; examples include the forces of nature, diseases, or injuries. Sin will always have great costs for us personally. Avoid these great costs and return to the True Savior of this world. Repeat the words of this prayer if you are at a loss for words:

Merciful Father, I have fallen into temptation and sin. I have sinned against You. I've turned my back on You and Your word. I have ruined the relationship You and I have built. It was a mistake to turn my back on You. Let not Your anger fall on me. My soul desires You again, Lord. I know You love me. Jeremiah 3:14 says You are married to the backslider and You will bring me to Zion. Rescue me and raise me up from this dark pit. Father, forgive me, and welcome me back home. I promise from this day forward to turn to You always, in the good and the bad, and prove my love for You. Thank You for Your grace and forgiveness. Thank You for releasing my guilt, knowing that there is no condemnation to those that believe in Jesus, and for healing my shame. In the mighty name of Jesus Christ I pray. Amen.

The "suddenly" moment comes upon you and there is nothing that can be done to stop it. Grace is the only truth that matters in this moment of time.

The report was told to my twin sister, whom I affectionately call Twinny, by a witness who was on the scene, while I was unconscious, awaiting emergency personnel to arrive. A young lady became aware of the accident, got out of her car and came and assessed the situation. She was moved with compassion after seeing two to three men trying to remove me from my vehicle because they thought it was going to explode. They pulled me out of the car and placed me on the scorching hot road. This compassionate stranger was then led to run to her car to grab a pillow and graciously placed it under my head until the paramedics got to me. She then grabbed and secured my belongings out of my car, including my iPhone, and was led to call the last two numbers I dialed on my phone. One call was placed to my beloved Grandma all the way in Anguilla, British West Indies, and the other was to a good friend named Blake in New York.

This act of kindness has left a lasting impression on me because she was a complete stranger and was not obligated to do anything for me. My phone was set to lock in thirty seconds; however, the stranger was able to dial the last two numbers called on my phone and alert them of the accident.

The question remains unanswered as to how in the world my phone was able to make a call outside of the thirty second time frame. I'm still in awe, but I believe with all my heart that it was grace at work, where the heavenly host of angels was on the scene, ensuring that everything needed in my incapacitation was done. This awesome young lady was then able to give my purse, Bible, shoes, and the awesome phone used to notify my love ones, to the emergency medical technicians to transport with me to whichever hospital they were taking me to. I ended up being transported to one of the major local trauma hospitals in the Atlanta area, which, by the way, did a really, awesome job.

My immediate relatives here in Atlanta knew I was in trouble when my precious Grandma and Blake called them and made them aware of my serious, life-threatening accident. As God ordained, my sister-in-law, Dr. Gumbs, whom I call Wandita, was one of the Chief Residents at the hospital I was taken to. She was then able to call one of the interns working with her at the hospital and was able to confirm that I was there by giving them my physical description. Having Dr. Gumbs there was a huge and significant support behind the scenes, and for that I am forever grateful.

You see, God knew on March 15, 2015, I would be at that trauma center, and it is no coincidence that my sister-in-law would be a Chief Resident at the same hospital at that exact date.

My friends and dear readers, our God will supply all our needs according to His riches in glory by Jesus Christ as written in Philippians 4:19. All of our needs means all. We cannot add to or subtract from this truth. Our Eternal God is faithful to all who call upon Him.

The Suddenly

Damaged car and the freight train

2
Good Always Comes Out of Bad

The neurosurgeons and the medical crew did not have any good news to give my family at the bedside. Their report from day one sounded terribly grim. They shared with my older brother, Kwesi Gumbs (whom I call Big Bro), and Wandita that due to the impact of the hit from the air bag to my head, my brain had started swelling and had caused some bleeding to occur, but they were doing all they could to stop the bleeding.

Meanwhile in St. Thomas, US Virgin Islands, Twinny, who was newly appointed as the Deputy Commissioner of the Health and Human Services Division, shared with her team that she had a family emergency and had to leave the island to be with her twin sister. She immediately booked a flight that Sunday night and was at my bedside by Monday night.

When Twinny arrived at the hospital, Big Bro (who is an Under Shepherd), my immediate Under Shepherd (Pastor Brown), and many others were at my bedside, rendering support through praying with family and friends. This ensured they received the spiritual support that was so needed at this uncertain and bleak time.

God often places you around His people, who in turn will be there for you in those tight places and spaces. I thank God for my church family also, who truly came and rendered support in whatever way they were led to. I now understand the realities of Under Shepherds, who fulfilled their due diligence and maintained the responsibility of feeding and protecting me during my unconsciousness.

The Bible uses the illustration of a shepherd and sheep many times because many people can easily identify with the context. A fascinating characteristic of sheep is their ability to instantly recognize the voice of their master.

While I was in an unconscious state of existence, my Under Shepherd would read and prophesy healing from the Word of God. My spirit recognized his voice and quickened under the power of the Word of God. In turn my physical body had to comply with what the Word of God said. John 10:27 (NIV) confirms this: *"My sheep listen to my voice; I know them, and they follow me."*

A good shepherd takes care of his sheep. Proper care entails feeding the entire flock by bringing them to good pasture, providing water, delivering new lambs, grooming them, leading them, training them to stay together, gathering the lost, wandering ones, and protecting the sheep in the field from those who prey. Each sheep needs the utmost protection because of their gentle nature and their innate need to follow.

We are all Under Shepherds and Jesus Christ is the Good Shepherd. We need to emulate what the Good Shepherd does for His sheep. I honor Pastor Brown and Big Bro today and I am forever grateful. 1 Thessalonians 5:12-13 (MSG) says, *"And now, friends, we ask you to honor those leaders who work so hard for you, who have been given the responsibility of urging and guiding you along in your obedience. Overwhelm them with appreciation and love."*

To those of you reading, do not be fooled; leaders in the Lord's church work very hard. I know because I am an ordained minister of the Gospel in the Lord's church. In addition to the regular activities such as planning and leading church services and prayer meetings, often times the leaders in the church are called upon to do other things. These things might include visiting the sick that are in the hospital or nursing home, attending community events, providing marriage counseling, burying the dead, performing weddings, and ministering to families that have lost their loved one. Leaders and Pastors have been called to do these things, but faithful prayers are a blessing and a source of strength to these men and women of God. Let us take a moment right now and pray for God's laborers:

> *Behold, how good and how pleasant it is for brethren to dwell together in unity. I pray that You, Lord, will provide strength to Your workers to carry out Your will. I pray for good and godly friends for my Pastor and ministers of the Gospel of Christ Jesus. Friendships that support their call to ministry. Friends that will allow them to relax yet hold them accountable as fellow Christians. Father, when they need time away from the ministry to enjoy family time, I pray that You will provide good friends that will be theirs for a lifetime and that they may dwell together with them in unity. Father, we pray that You keep them all humble, always relying upon You, and that You'll give them Your perfect gift of wisdom and direction that is needed. We thank you for providing the support that is needed. In Jesus' name we pray. Amen.*

Big Bro ensured that I had twenty-four hours, around-the-clock support. They planned, purposed, and scheduled themselves around the clock, ensuring that I was never alone. The power of presence was and is quite crucial. I now understand the awesome power of presence and how God uses it to bring healing to the sick in many ways.

That's right - it is simple, yet the impact is immeasurable. After the day of Pentecost, the disciples became very skilled at healing. So many of the sick had been healed that people brought out their sick and laid them in the street, hoping that the shadow of the apostles would fall on them:

"And believers were increasingly added to the Lord, multitudes of both men and women, so that they brought the sick out into the streets and laid them on beds and couches, that at least the shadow of Peter passing by might fall on some of them."
Acts 5:14-15 (NKJV)

We have also read in the Bible many times that power went out from Jesus as He passed through a crowd, and the sick were healed. This also happened in the case of the woman with the issue of blood found in Luke 8: 43-48. She touched the hem of His garment, and immediately Jesus felt virtue leave Him. The woman who had suffered for twelve years, who had spent all she had on physicians, immediately was made whole.

Often times some of us carry God's presence in a way that releases healing without our awareness and without a single word being said. There is power in presence. My brother, sister-in-law, Twinny, and all my immediate siblings, cousins, and church members who watched over me twenty-four hours a day, all have an intimate knowledge of the saving grace and healing power of Jesus Christ. The presence of Christ in their lives administered my healing because His spirit dwells in them after they became born again. Let me pray for those who are reading. We pray that you may yearn for His presence in your lives:

Compassionate Father, I pray that You will visit us today and make Your presence known in our lives. I pray that those around me may be affected by Your presence.

Whether it be for healing or for strength. I pray that those around me may look upon me and see that I have been with You. Let Your Glory surround me like a glove.

Give me faith to believe that You can change the atmosphere and those around me through prayer and through acts of love and compassion. Let Your Kingdom come on earth as it is in heaven. Help me to cultivate Your presence in my life. I choose to partner with You for transformation in my home, my workplace, and the nation.

In the Mighty name of Jesus I pray. Amen.

3
Delayed But Not Denied

The grim reports continued to come in. On the second day, the report noted that I was having a hard time breathing on my own and that I needed assistance. It was decided on day number two to put me on a mechanical breathing machine known as a ventilator.

Looking back at this truth makes me so grateful for this awesome blessing known to us as breathing. What comes so easy for some of us can be in an instant life or death for so many others. Also, in this unconscious state of being, the doctors inserted a gastrostomy tube in the left upper quadrant of my stomach to assist in providing nutrition to me through a feeding tube, seeing that I was not able to do this on my own.

Thirty days prior to my date with destiny, I had started a new job as the Health Services Administrator at an incredible facility and did not have second thoughts about my health insurance coverage when I was in between jobs. I have done this a few times before. My former employer normally has thirty days to notify the plan administrator about a qualifying event entitling me to health insurance coverage. It was day 30. Big Bro learned that I did not have an active insurance plan, so he immediately enrolled me in the COBRA plan offered by my former employer. What a Mighty God we serve.

My COBRA plan covered the cost of over $600,000.00 dollars in medical expenses. I shudder to think of where I would be now without this insurance plan and the timing of my COBRA eligibility with the accident. So here is the major announcement from someone who has been there and was caught almost without coverage. Please, please enroll in whichever COBRA plan your employer provides during transition from the old to the new job, because you never know what the next second will bring your way. Take it from a sincere source. If I had known what March 15, 2015 would bring I would have been better prepared.

The results from multiple scans of my brain still showed swelling and bleeding on my brain. The doctors came to the same conclusion time and time again…. that I might not survive. That was day number two. On day number three some doctors came into my room and informed Twinny that I had been diagnosed with a Diffuse Axonal Injury (DAI). This type of injury causes everything in the person's life to change.

Diffuse Axonal Injury (DAI) is a brain injury in which extensive lesions in white matter tracts occur over a widespread area. DAI is one of the most common and devastating types of traumatic brain injury and is a major cause of unconsciousness and persistent vegetative state after severe head trauma.

It occurs in about half of all cases of severe head trauma and may be the primary damage that occurs in concussions. The outcome is frequently coma, with over ninety percent of patients with severe DAI never regaining consciousness. Those who do wake up often remain significantly impaired.

The doctors continued to report that I could end up in a vegetative state and would not be able to do anything for myself, "but," they reiterated, "we are doing everything we can." So, after giving this sad report, they left the room.

After the doctors left the room, Twinny, like a warrior on the battle field, immediately went into prayer, refusing to accept that report. She confidently reminded ABBA Father that He is the Great Physician over the countless natural physicians in the trauma center where we were and that He had the final say in Kenza's current situation. The Word of God says that we should "approach the throne of grace with confidence, so that we may receive mercy and find grace to help us in our time of need." (Hebrews 4:16). She shared with me that she reminded Father that Kenza had not done all the things prophesied over her to do. She also called Big Bro and gave the despairing report.

I am certain that Big Brother, who many times before ended our conversations with a word of prayer for issues that were of less significance, petitioned God on my behalf. Whose report will you believe? (Isaiah 53). Verse 5 of the same chapter later reads, *"But He was wounded for our transgressions, He was bruised for our iniquities: the chastisement of our peace was upon Him; and with His stripes we are healed."*

My Pastor and other visitors that visited me that day heard the grim report as well. But all who got the report, refused to believe that this was going to be my portion. They chose to believe the report of the Lord.

When Big Bro realized what I was up against, he got my other sisters and mother, who lived in the Virgin Islands, on the telephone and devised a plan of visitations. He planned visits to Atlanta around each other's time to ensure there was no overlapping and that my twenty-four-hour care would continue. And that plan happened smoothly. Big Bro understood the power of presence. Yes, even though

I was not physically aware of these happenings, I was being supported big time by Mi Familia.

On day five my older Sister Anuska, whom we lovingly call Nuxie, her husband, and her son travelled from St. Thomas, US Virgin Islands, to see me that Thursday and were with me for ten days. Nuxie shared she was not expecting to see me in the state I was in because whenever she spoke to Big Bro, he would always say, "Kenza is doing good". When she got there that Thursday night, she was filled with uncertainty because the severity of the physical damage was very evident. She admitted that the thought crossed her mind that all her siblings would have to alternate taking care of me.

Being the analytical person that she is, she also began asking the nurses lots of questions, who again gave depressing reports based on their medical expertise. She told me that the nurse on duty said that the damage was as if my entire brain had shifted in my head from the impact and persons with these types of injuries normally do not recover.

What we later realized was that whenever Big Bro spoke to Nuxie or was updating the rest of the family, he was exercising incredible faith. He always said, "It is well." It reminds me of the story in the Bible of the Shunammite woman in 2 Kings 4: 8-16.

This Shunammite woman had a need and was desperate for God's promise. She was childless and her husband was quite old. You know the Bible is full of the promises of God, but it is up to each one of us to read, identify, and claim the promises that God has so freely given us.

The prophet, Elisha, gave the Shunammite woman a promise under the authority of God. Like many prophets, he spoke for God. Elisha told the woman that she would soon have a son. She knew that Elisha was a man of God, a prophet, but she still did not believe in her heart that she would have a child. God had promised the Shunammite woman a son through the spoken word of Elisha, and she had him. God does NOT lie and He keeps all His promises. *Numbers 23:19 NKJV - "God is not a man, that He should lie, nor a son of man that He should repent. Has He said, and will He not do? Or has He spoken, and will He not make it good?"* The son that the woman was promised was now lying dead in her arms.

If the Shunammite woman and Big Bro had looked at things through their natural eyes, she would have accepted the death of her child, and Big Bro would have accepted my diagnosis and grim reports. But she knew that God had promised her a son, and she knew that her promise would not be taken back by God. The woman took her promise that was "dead" and secluded it in a room where no one would interfere and closed the door. In seclusion there was no one to discourage her by saying,

"Surely you see that your son is dead - there is nothing else that can be done." She determined that she would seek out the man of God on behalf of her "dead" promise.

Sometimes God gives us a promise, and it seems like the promise is dead or improbable. We need to be like the Shunammite woman; we need to shut out the things and people that might keep our promise dead. We must be very careful of what we hear and whom we listen to concerning our promise.

There is life and death in our words. *Proverbs 18:21 (NKJV) - "Death and life are in the power of the tongue, and those who love it will eat its fruit."* Every word that comes out of man's mouth either brings life or it brings death. The words we say are very powerful. God spoke the world into existence: "By faith we understand that the universe was created by the word of God, so that what is seen was not made out of things that are visible." Hebrews 11:3

And God said, "Let there be light," and there was light (Genesis 1:3). Words will either bless a situation or curse it. By putting the son in the room away from everyone, she was protecting her promise from words of death. We, too, must hold on to the promise(s) that God has given us and shield the promise(s) and ourselves from the words of naysayers. We need to focus on what the Word of God says. His promises are Yea and Amen.

During these times we must only listen to and trust in what God has to say, not man. We serve a God who cannot fail. He is "The Rock! His work is perfect, for all His ways are justice; A God of truth and without injustice, Righteous and upright is He." Deuteronomy 32:4 (NKJV). We serve a God of completion.

By the seventh day in the creation process, God completed the work which He had started. His works are nothing short of perfection. All of God's works are good. He never leaves anything half done. When God created the heavens and the earth, God saw all that he had made, and it was very good.

He never gives us something just to take it away again. We must not waver in our faith even when we do not see the answer with our natural eyes. We must not waver in our faith even though the wait may seem to us like an eternity. No matter how hard things get, or how bad things look, or how negative the doctor's report is, you should and must still rejoice - not rejoicing for what you are going through but rejoicing, knowing that the Lord God Almighty is on our side and the battle has already been won.

We can graciously rejoice, knowing that God will never leave us or forsake us. Big Bro was like the Shunammite woman, never wavering in his faith and always saying to my sister and all who asked about Kenza, "It is well."

Here is a prayer of faith in times of trouble found in Psalm 31:1-5 NKJV: By the director of music himself - A psalm of David.

"In you, Lord, I put my trust; let me never be ashamed; Deliver me in Your righteousness. Bow down Your ear to me. Deliver me speedily; Be my rock of refuge, A fortress of defense to save me. Therefore, for Your name's sake, lead and guide me. Pull me out of the net which they have secretly laid for me. For You are my strength. Into Your hand I commit my spirit; You have redeemed me, O Lord God of truth."

Your hand of love is guiding me to Your peace. I am in a whirlwind of confusion right now, but even this storm cannot hold back the blessings from You. Your lovingkindness is better than life. I thank You for divine revelations. You are motivating me to get through this difficult time. I will not fear. I will not be dismayed. I will not let my heart be troubled. Like Jabez said in the Word of God: Lord, increase my faith and enlarge my territory. I choose to believe the promises of God. Thank you, Father. In Jesus' name I pray. Amen.

Despite my fragile state of existence, my dear family far away, such as those who were in Alabama, Washington, DC, Maryland, Anguilla British West Indies, St. Thomas US Virgin Islands, and St. Martin/Maarten, encouraged my dear family members who were witnessing this state of my being first hand. This incident proved to me for sure that our God is indeed a very present help in times of trouble, and He will always provide the help, support, and whatever else is needed in abundance.

ABBA Father, thank you for being faithful in the most uncertain times of our lives! Faithful and upright You are.

4
The Number of Completion

Going into the seventh day, I finally opened my eyes. The number seven is often referenced in the Bible as a number that signifies completion. It derives much of its meaning from being tied directly to God's creation of all things. There are seven days in a week and God's Sabbath is on the seventh day.

My comatose state had come to its end on the seventh day. Twinny was in the room with me and was able to witness and celebrate with me. She called everyone to share the great news. Kenza's eyes were opened, but I still was not able to speak. My speech was interrupted because of the sustained head injury.

Nuxie shared that when she learned I had opened my eyes, she headed straight to the hospital. When she came into my room to see me, she asked me if I knew who she was. I shook my head nodding yes, but when her husband walked into the room, I greeted him with the biggest grin, one that stretched from ear to ear. She joked that she was temporarily hurt that she did not receive the same grin, but seeing that my brain had suffered major injuries, she decided to forgive me, but she would never let me forget it.

Twinny was moved to capture some of these tender moments through pictures, which truly showed this state in live form at the beginning of this nine month recovery journey, although I was not even aware of these happenings. In some of the pictures, my eyes were open, but there was this glazed look on my face, like I was somewhere hundreds of miles away. But the physical and spiritual support that I so needed was there indeed and there in one hundred percent swing. It is an amazing truth that a picture is worth a thousand words, and I am here to say that this is the remarkable truth, truly.

Pictures that brought tears to my eyes; tears of joy.

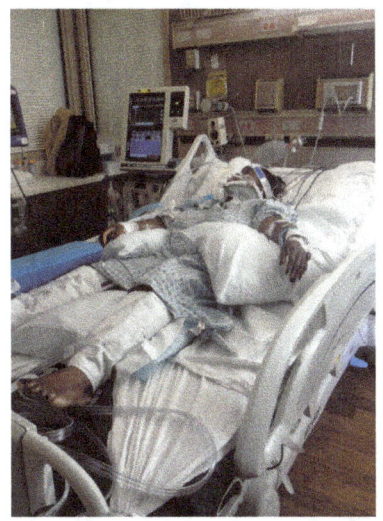
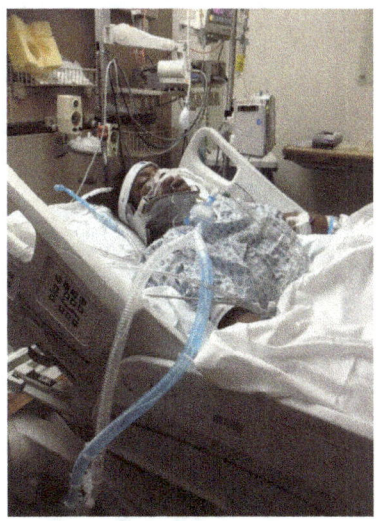

Kenza Gumbs *Kenza Gumbs*

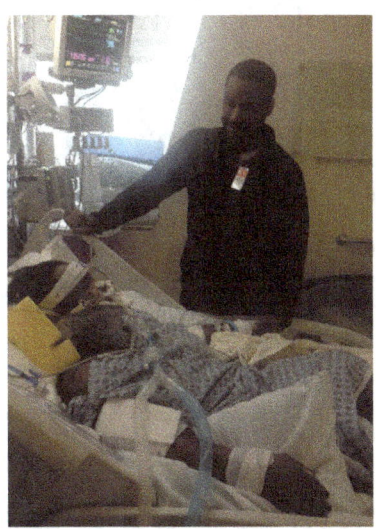
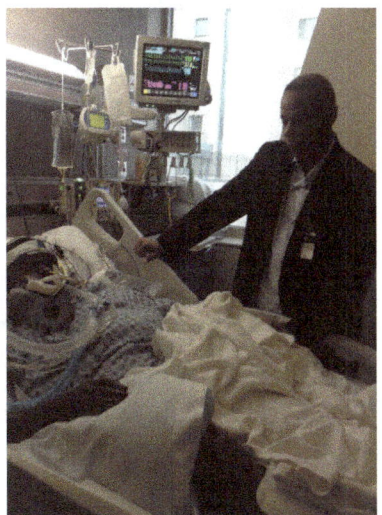

Big Bro and his Overseer, Pastor Ray, rendering much needed support. I'm forever grateful to Father God and His Under Shepherds.

Pictures that brought tears to my eyes; tears of joy.

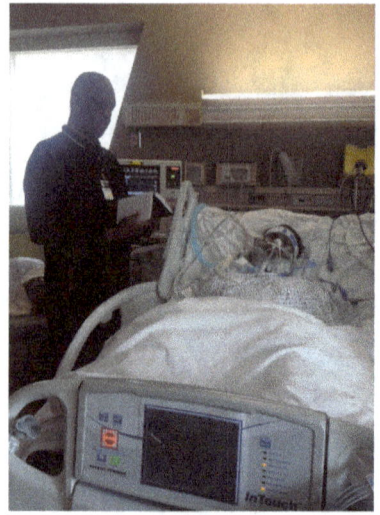

*Under Shepherd,
Pastor Brown*

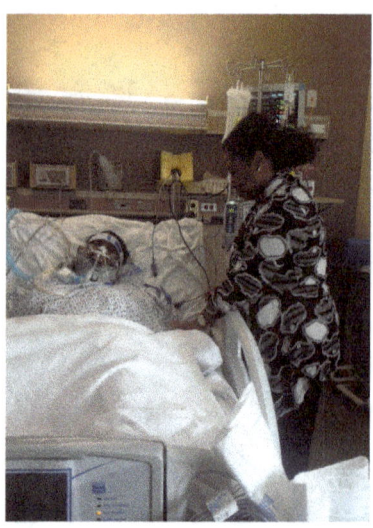

*Under Shepherd
Pastor Blanding*

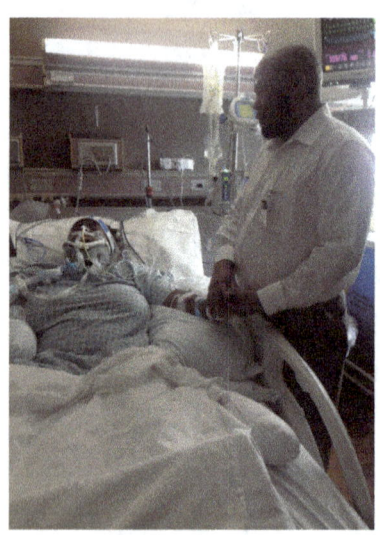

Deacon Bernard

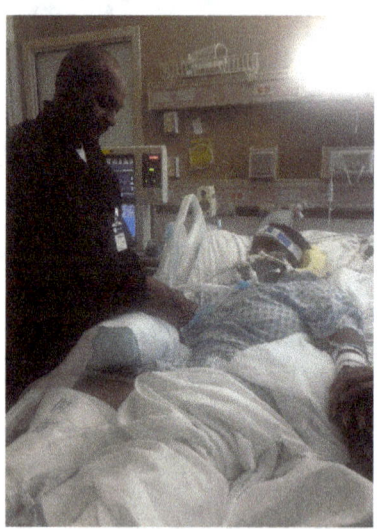

Deacon Avery

The Number of Completion

Pictures that brought tears to my eyes; tears of joy.

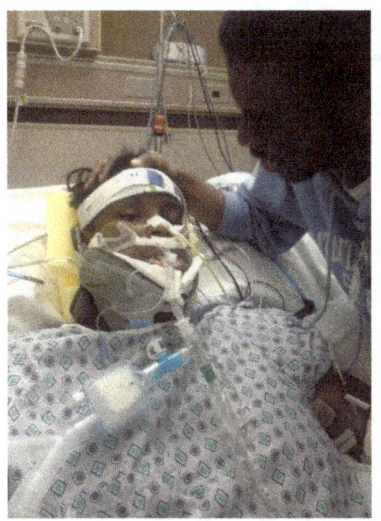

Deacon Rashaad

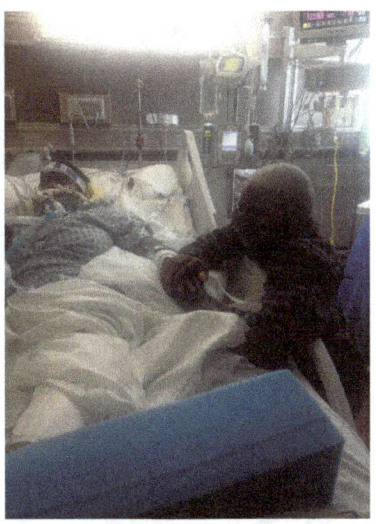

Brother Larris

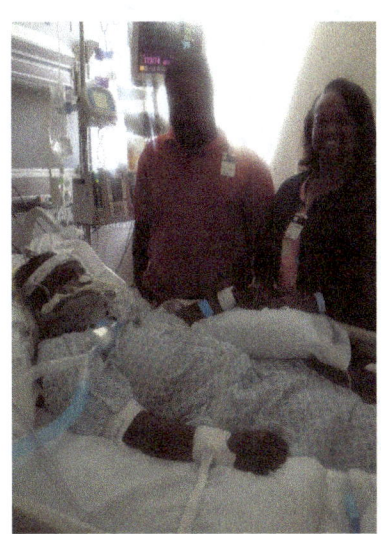

Brother and Sister Campbell

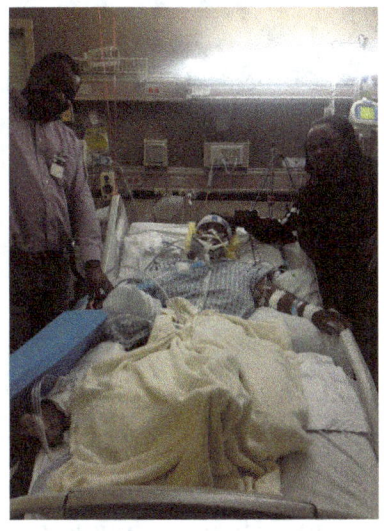

Elders James and Lorraine Richardson

Pictures that brought tears to my eyes; tears of joy.

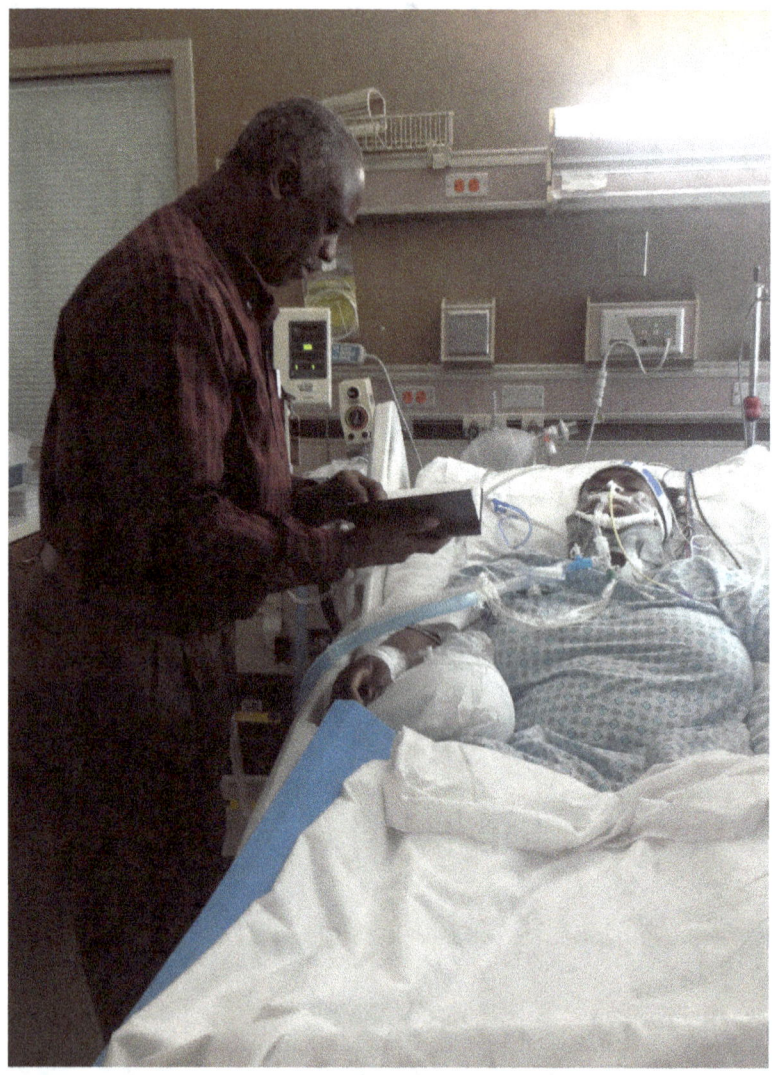

Under Shepherd, Pastor Brown, with his famous black book. He is feeding my spirit, the Word of the living God, which brought healing and strength to my bones.

The Number of Completion

Pictures that brought tears to my eyes; tears of joy.

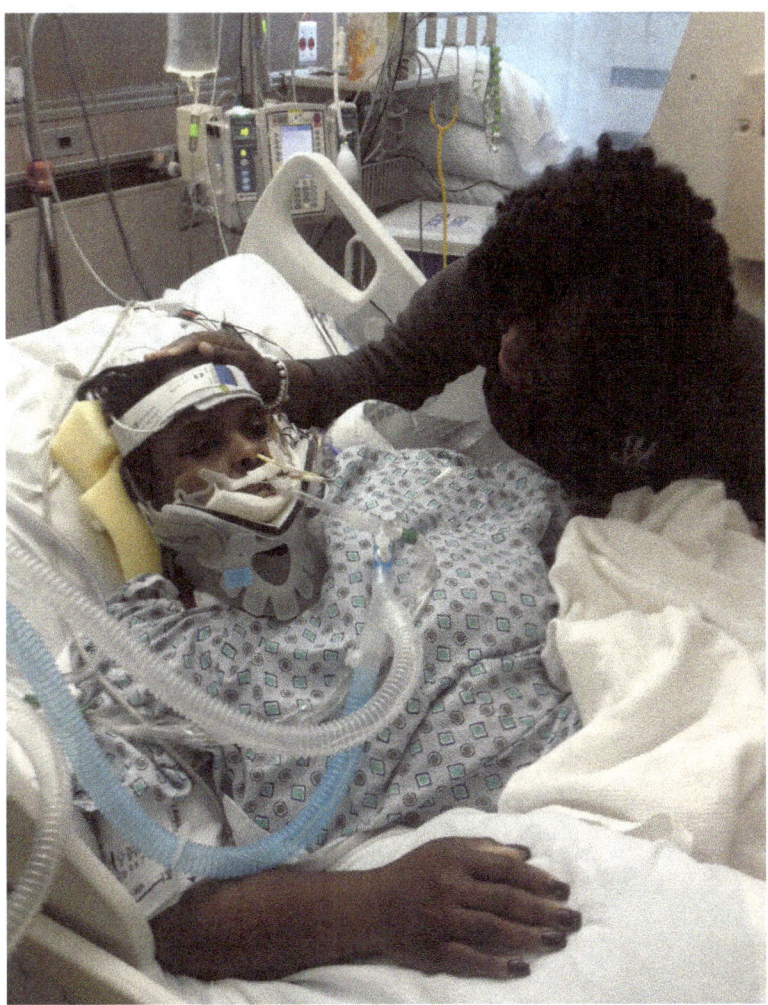

Twinny (my twin) and I are two of a kind. I tell you, God always knows what we need, and He provides it for us. Twinny and I, no matter what happens to either of us, just love each other free of conditions and always have supported each other beyond human understanding. I am eternally grateful to have come into this world with her. Praises to ABBA Father.

Pictures that brought tears to my eyes; tears of joy.

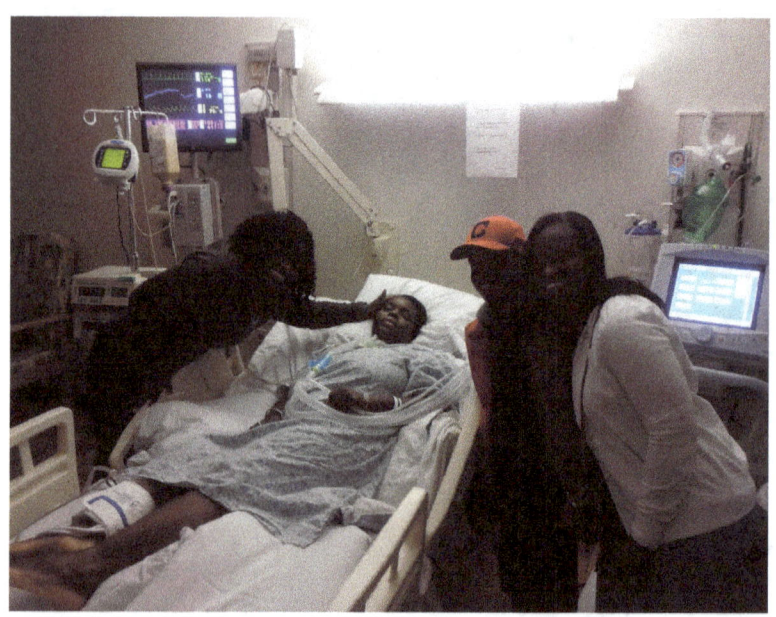

Twinny, Nuxie, and Kaden showing some love to me after I said my first word, "Amen."

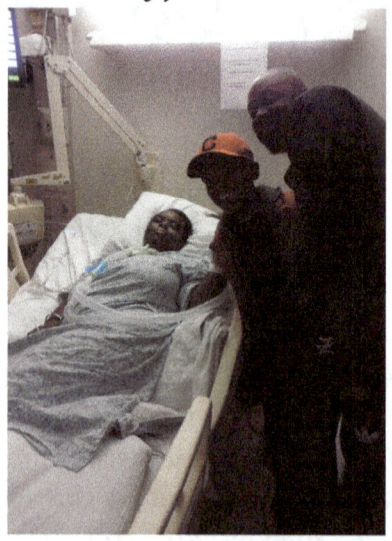

Kwame and Kaden

The Number of Completion

The medical report updates kept coming in quite negative and very dim. The medical team on this day, day number twelve, attempted to wean me off the ventilator to assess if I was able to breathe on my own, but I was still having a tough time doing that. It was then decided to place a tracheostomy tube in my neck to assist me with the airway deficiency that was presenting itself.

Twinny reported to Wandita when she learned of this news; they both prayed and cried for me and mourned with me even though I was not able to cry with them. The surgery was completed the next day, and I was then able to breathe much better as determined by improved blood gases tests and improved oxygen saturation levels. I was no longer having trouble breathing; the time came for my lungs to rest.

Let me take a moment and give a shout- out to all the men and women in the faith who are intercessors. It is an awesome calling to stand in the gap for others. It is an awesome privilege and such an honor to approach God's throne for someone else in times when their faith is hanging on the edge. I encourage you today, don't give up, knowing that we serve a faithful God who will reward us for our faithfulness in praying for each other.

Let us pray for the intercessors at this time:

Loving God, we thank You now for all Your chosen intercessors who intercede for the needs of others. We thank You that Jesus Christ is the Chief Intercessor, making intercession for us all. Father, may intercessors understand the Scripture found in Ephesians 6:12-13 (NKJV). "For we do not wrestle against flesh and blood, but against principalities, against powers, against the rulers of the darkness of this age, against spiritual hosts of wickedness in the heavenly places. Therefore, take up the whole armor of God, that you may be able to withstand in the evil day, and having done all, to stand." May they stand in Your truth and power, while interceding for brothers and sisters. In Jesus' name we pray. Amen.

5
Set Times And Seasons For Everything

At about the twenty-ninth day, I was transferred to a rehabilitation center that specialized in spinal cord and brain injury rehabilitation along with focusing on brain research.

This facility is among the top ten rehabilitation hospitals in our nation. My Familia was given the awesome opportunity to apply for a scholarship that would help incur some of the costs of my rehabilitation, and it brings me great joy to share that we were awarded monies that were applied to my treatment stay.

Thank God for loving grandmothers. My Grandma called Twinny every day, sometimes even multiple times in a day, depending on what was going on. In the first week of my rehabilitation stay, one morning Grandma asked Twinny to put the phone next to my ear while she prayed and sang to me.

It was at the end of Grandma's prayer that I uttered my first word, and that word was "AMEN!" Twinny immediately called Big Bro, who called my older sister, who called another sister. You see within five minutes all my immediate family celebrated this milestone with me, saying my first word.

The long - awaited - for word finally happened with an "Amen," meaning, "It is so." My spirit was certainly agreeing with whatever Grandma had asked our Lord and Savior for. My precious family shared with me, after I was able to utter some words, that my famous question was, "Why did this happen to me?" I had a million and two "whys" and I asked the same question repeatedly. They all lovingly told me that they did not have an answer for me, but they believed that God would reveal the "whys" at the appointed time.

This is a reminder for all who at times forget, our Great God is a God of seasons and times. Ecclesiastes 3:1 says it oh so delicately: "To everything there is a season, a time for every purpose under heaven." Seasons which accompany times come and go; they have a beginning and an end. We sincerely need to know and understand that the Great God we serve carries out His plans in seasons and set times. We are synchronized with His timing whether we want to accept it or not.

When trying to understand what is going on in our lives, it helps to plug into the knowledge of what season it is. God's chronological time clock ticks forward within seasons of winter, spring, summer, and fall. Chronos refers to clock time or time that can be measured, for example, seconds, minutes, hours, and years.

His Kairos clock is not defined in seconds, minutes, hours, weeks, months, and years but is measured by the right, opportune moments or better yet the supreme moment that ticks forward in the supernatural realm.

This shifts our understanding of the spiritual realities and our awareness. Chronologically, I was now in a winter season, but spring was on the horizon. Spring is a season when God brings us to and gives us new beginnings, fresh starts, promotions, birthing of new ministries, natural birthing of babies, jobs, and new assignments.

There is a time of refreshing that comes upon us in the Kairos appointed times. Just like in the Kairos time, chronologically spring comes, and it is a time of refreshing or "conception". We begin to see the first spiritual growth of what God spoke in our winter. It is a time of resurrection power, a time of hope, love, courage, and passion. God promises to reveal my answer and your answer in the fullness of time.

The time on the calendar came for Twinny to return home. She was able to spend the first four weeks after my "date" with me, and she cherished them all. It was now time for my younger sister, Shamika, whom I call Shambuka, to make her rotation. It was now her time to come up and spend time with her ailing big sister.

Shambuka shared that she was put on guard by Nuxie, who told her I was doing a little better, but I was not okay. Shambuka relayed to me I was understanding what she and others would say because I nodded my head and voiced short word phrases like yes, no, etc. I was still not as vocal as she would have liked. She shared I became confused at times. I learned that I asked her my favorite question that I so freely asked everyone who came to see me. Why did this happen to me? She as well tried to answer the best way she could.

At the end of her three weeks stay with me, I had improved significantly compared to the first day she saw me. As a matter of fact, she shared I moved from being slow in speech and movement to doing things that the doctors said might not happen.

The doctors marveled at my recovery. I had made such an improvement that my nursing training had kicked in, and I was noticing that some of the staff were not doing their due diligence in washing their hands, and I was not happy about that.

It was now my dear mother's turn to visit. She sacrificed everything that she was doing in St. Thomas to come to Atlanta to ensure that I had the help I needed on this long road to recovery. Shambuka was able to show Mother around the rehabilitation center and orient her to where everything like the laundry room, cafeteria, and the library were located.

At Shambuka's departure, the physical therapist was working with me to regain the so needed strength in my right side which was grossly weakened due to the extent of my injury. I thank God that though my physical body had major injuries, not one bone in my body was broken. My cousins, Shakiem, whom I call Shaka, and Rashaad (Shaady), who ate lunch with me on that destined day, were also able to spend time with me on the weekends, allowing Mother to take some breaks.

My beloved Uncle Alphonso whom I call Uncle Al, was very supportive, driving up to Atlanta from Alabama to support his Familia. My uncle and mother are extremely close, so he was coming up to hang out with his big sister and visit his ailing niece. As time progressed, I finally was able to understand sentences and make sense of what people were saying to me and provide responses that were correct through writings and much better verbal responses.

My speech therapist recommended that at this time I keep a book and a pen with me always to aid in better communication tactics.

My penmanship wasn't the best, but I was determined to put my words on paper when I was not able to vocalize my thoughts because at times I really wanted to get my point or points across, the good ones and the not so good ones.

I became more aware over the course of a few weeks and boy, oh boy, this period sure did feel like I was trapped in a body that was not doing what I wanted it to do. My entire right side was affected. I am right- handed, so you can only imagine how that was. The human brain is not the biggest organ in the body, but it sure does control every part of the body, and it is only when it is not functioning at its optimal that are you then able to appreciate what it does for you indeed.

I needed lots of assistance with feeding myself even though they had started me on a pureed diet. I also could not walk on my own because my entire right side was extremely weak, so I became dependent on a wheel chair that was able to move me here and there. I had finally built up enough strength to push myself. I remember not being able to take a shower on my own and having the Certified Nursing Assistants (CNA's) assisting me in performing this duty.

Set Times And Seasons For Everything

This was a very humbling experience; never in a million-years did I ever think I would be the patient and have someone else assisting me in the activities of daily living aka ADL's, but here I was in a state of existence I did not expect to be in but was in. Thank God the showers were not every day, I had to shower but was scheduled to shower two to three times a week up until the time I went home. Any other given time I would have been insisting that I shower each day, but I was actually happy that baths were not daily.

It is truly incredible how the human body, once interrupted, does wonders for you. I must mention this awesome fact that I absolutely loved. I had no menstrual cycle for about four to five months. When my cycle did return, it started with three-day cycles, then progressed to four-day cycles, then normal five-day cycles. Now looking back, I loved every second of it, well minus the pain and all the other tough stuff. You young ladies of childbearing age who are reading my story, can agree with this, for sure.

Days turned into nights and nights into days. The recovery period was long and difficult. On some nights I remember crying myself to sleep with so many questions on my mind. Yes, I was busy asking the Lord my multiple "why" questions again; Questions such as "Why did you allow me to go through this, Lord"? "You should have told me something, Lord"? "Am I ever going to get better, Lord"? "If I ever get better, will I be the same, Lord"?

It was to these questions that I got not one single answer. However, my spirit was comforted with God's Shalom, where He reminded me, He will never leave me and will never forsake me. I relied on those comforting words especially the word "never."

The word "never" was ever so dear to me, and this word allowed me to trust and depend on Him completely. I was also comforted by the Christian hymn written by Joseph M. Scriven in 1855 to comfort his mother who was living in Ireland while he was in Canada entitled "What a friend we have in Jesus." The lyrics go on to read "All our sins and griefs to bear, what a privilege to carry, everything to God in prayer." This song brought peace to my heart during those long recovery days and nights.

My present battle was the many mood swings I experienced as a side effect from the medications. My attending physician, who got reports from the team that my mood had changed, started me on Prozac. There were times when my mood came with ups and downs. I was not a fan of medication, but I went along with it.

My ear nose and throat doctor also started me on some low dose Prednisone to keep my lungs free of inflammation. Boy, if anyone had told me this medication would make me the meanest person at times, I would have said, "You are crazy." But because my lungs needed it, I was subjected to it although it affected me hormonally big time.

There were some incredible inpatient therapists at the rehabilitation center, that took care of me - the occupational, physical, and speech therapists, to be exact. The counselors and the nursing staff were great as well, but I had some not so good ones also. I will not call any names or titles, but I am hoping that they will read this book and change for themselves and, most importantly, for the patients who are depending on them to do their job and do it well. I recall this incident where an attendant's bedside manner was particularly extremely unprofessional. One afternoon I needed suctioning of my tracheostomy, so when the attendant came into my room, it seemed like he/she was having a tough time and was in a rush. I was still not able to talk fluently at this time, but during the suctioning, which was quite tender to me, I waved my hand letting the individual know the suctioning must stop. This request infuriated the individual, who rudely asked me to let it be known when I wanted them to do their job. I wrote on a piece of paper saying to this person, "Yes, I want you to do your job but gently, please." I guess that was not the response that they wanted and in the most disrespectful tone responded that they did not have time for me.

Big Bro, who normally does not get flustered easily, also asked the individual, "What is the problem?" Without uttering a reply, they left the room. Normally on any other day, I would have called the supervisor or manager and made a complaint report, but I was so exhausted that I did not even have the strength to make the complaint. But, boy oh boy, I asked the Lord to keep me from behaving like that if He was to raise me back up again off my sick bed to take care of His sick people.

In caring for the sick, compassion to the tenth degree is necessary. Always remember but for the grace of God there go I. We must be intentional to sow seeds of love, caring, patience, peace, and all the pure and perfect gifts that come down from above and be God's conduits that bring peace and joy to the sick, whether it be sickness of the body, mind, or soul.

6
Tell The Truth And Shame The Devil

One day at a therapy session my therapist said to me, "You are so lucky to be alive." I reflected on the goodness of God and was able to adamantly affirm on my paper that it was not luck. I stressed that if it was up to luck I would be dead; it sure was not luck that did this for me, it was God and Him only.

Having received this response from me, she looked at me all flushed in the face and said, "Oh yeah, it is a miracle". I looked her right in her eyes and said, "Yes, He is a miracle- working God." After that precious moment, she understood she was not permitted to say anything to me about luck. I was not timid about giving praise to God for keeping me in the land of the living, even though I was quite wounded and now in full recovery mode.

After a few weeks of therapy, I was still not

walking as balanced as I should. It was during these times that I became uncertain and anxious with thoughts of falling. Sometimes I became quite unsure if I could go through with therapy.

Yes, here was the Preacher woman, or should I say Minister, here was the Health Services Administrator, or should I say the healthcare leader, and here was the brave one; yes, here was Kenza Chanice Gumbs with thoughts of not being able to make it up this huge mountain that was set before me. With these twirling thoughts racing in my head, I asked God for peace, and as always, His presence came and quieted my mind.

My Comforter surrounded me and ended these wild thoughts, bringing my mind to rest. Each believer in Christ is expected to get to know God better as we walk the pilgrim's pathway. Yes, there are truths that we will only learn through suffering and hardship. One of those truths is that He is the God of all comfort.

We will discover God as Comforter in Psalm 46, which begins with the following words: "God is our refuge and strength, a very present help in trouble." As we approach the end of the psalm, God is speaking to every heart reading this scripture as He says, "Be still, and know that I am God" (v. 10). Times of trouble are quite confusing, and we want to do something to change the happenings, but it is in these times that God requires us to be silent.

We must learn that days filled with suffering and sorrow give us the opportunity to be silent. These can be precious moments of quiet reflection when God speaks to us. Rest assured if we do not set aside some time each day to be silent before God, then He has His own way of setting us aside.

If we take advantage of these periods of quiet solitude, we too can increase in the knowledge of God. The Christian who is suffering needs a special kind of comfort that only God can give. As our loving Comforter, He stands by our side to lead us to our "Gilead" to find the soothing balm that will heal our sin sick souls.

There was a big choice before me. I had to choose whether I would go through the door of accepting what was happening to me or not go through the door. I am happy to admit that I chose to go through the acceptance door and took it all in with some deep breaths and rested in God's solitude. I made up my mind, saying, "Lord, your word tells me I can speak to any mountain and command it to move and it must move," and yes, even with the mustard seed size faith, I had to believe, and I did believe. With a deep breath I said, "Mountain, get out of my way, in Jesus' mighty name." We need to stand in the liberty that Jesus has provided for all of us, His children. I was then able to sleep peacefully since that day.

Mornings at the rehabilitation center began with getting myself together with assistance from staff so I could be ready and down to breakfast between 7:30 and 8:00 a.m. I was still getting nutrition from being tube - fed at night for seven to eight hours. It is amazing how you adapt to food even in a pureed form. After having a bland but nutritious pureed breakfast, I was off to my scheduled therapy sessions.

Every day I was so happy to see my bed at the end of therapy. Just getting ready for my day took so much out of me, but looking back at it all, I can say it was nothing but the grace of God that kept me grounded. I was able to go through each session with notable improvements. My therapists did a great job of encouraging me with verbal reports where they shared I was getting better.

Each day lunch came like clockwork. When that was finished, I went on to the next therapy session and finally back to dinner. At times, despite making the choice to accept these happenings in my life, there were some isolated periods where I became extremely discouraged. My attending doctor wanted to prescribe Aricept for my immediate short-term memory loss, but again, because I was not a fan of medication, I was quite skeptical at first. She had me start the medication at night.

After about two weeks or so she increased my dose. It was in these fragile moments that my dear Mother did her best to keep me encouraged and grounded with some much-needed and welcomed pep talks, and, yes, with some tears flowing and feeling sorry for myself, I persevered. Healing is the children's bread, and at times this truth needs to be spoken out loud, so the enemy of our souls can hear the truth and release his hold upon us.

If I was not a Registered Nurse and knew the benefits of the tube, boy, oh boy, I shudder to think of what I would have done with that tube. I could only imagine how others coped with this "lovely" tube in the neck.

Before my accident, I enjoyed sleeping on my stomach but that came to a screeching halt. Not only was it impossible for me to sleep on my belly, it was impossible for me to sleep in any other position lower than that of a sixty to ninety degree angle. When I tried to sleep in a lower position, my head would begin to get so dizzy that I would feel overwhelmingly sick. I could not wait for this tube to come out of my neck, but I was in for a quite a journey before that happened.

We are now on the first day of May 2015, and so much was to happen in this month. I was to be discharged from inpatient rehabilitation, transitioned to outpatient rehabilitation, and my younger cousin Shaka, was graduating from Southern Polytech. This was awesome because Grandma and Auntie were going to be able to "kill two birds with one stone". Meaning they were able to get to see me during my recovery as well as attend Shak's graduation. On the evening when family landed in Atlanta, they came straight to the rehabilitation center to give me some love and support. It was great seeing Grandma and Auntie again, so soon from my December 2014 visit.

I was to be discharged on Friday and Shak was to graduate on Saturday. It was a bitter-sweet moment for me because I wanted to attend Shak's graduation, but when I considered the heat and the length of the graduation ceremony, I was in no physical state to attend. For the entire four years of his undergraduate studies, Shak worshipped with me at The Corner, and I wanted to support him like he had done with me so many times.

The day finally came to be discharged. I made sure I had gotten phone numbers and email addresses of my new acquaintances that I wanted to stay in touch with. I was given my discharge papers with all the must do's and don'ts. It was a hallelujah shout for me.

I was told by my physical therapist during my

last therapy session that I was one of the first patients with a traumatic brain injury (also known as a TBI) that had walked out of rehabilitation without being in a wheel chair or having a walking device or anything else to support me, and for that I am forever grateful. Friday, May 7, 2015, was significant for me. I now have a firsthand in-depth understanding of how patients feel when they are being discharged from a hospital or rehab because I lived it. Big Bro drove Mother and me home on that highly anticipated day.

Upon arriving home, to my surprise, I spoke to my Dad who was so happy to speak with me, that his joy turned into tears. Dad was extremely apologetic towards me and said he was so sorry that he could not be by my side. I reassured him that, through grace, Mother and my other family members were there with me, and we will be ok. He finally sounded like he came to peace about the happenings and accepted that he was not able to be there with me. I had never in my whole life heard my Dad cry, but I finally heard the cry from his heart and, for the first time in my life, I was consoling him. I reminded him that my life was in God's hands and he was not to worry. We were able to play catch- up on a few things and have rebuilt a solid relationship ever since. Love you, Dad.

Here is another part of my awesome testimony about God's provision. Thirty days before my accident, I purchased a Volkswagen Beetle as a second car. My plan was to use it to drive to work Monday through Friday. The new car I had was about eleven months old, and I had already put close to twenty thousand miles on it. I was led to purchase my second car with the thought that I was not going to put too much mileage on my new vehicle. Thirty days later my new car was declared a total loss.

It is in times like these, you become ever so thankful for a second car. It is truly mysterious how that worked out, but it did. Another awesome part of my testimony was that Mother was able to drive the six-speed turbo engine that came with the car. The Volkswagen Beetle was the benefit of being obedient to the heart's tug, and that truly worked out for me when it was all said and done.

I do not know what you may be going through right now, but rest assured our Mighty God provides. It is no coincidence you are reading this book right now.

Let us pray:

We thank You that there is no situation that is so terrible that You, Eternal God, cannot remedy. For You are Jehovah-Jireh, the God Who provides. We thank You that You own it all and hold everything in Your hands. We thank You that You know our needs before we even ask, before we even come to You. You are aware of all that concerns us, and You have a plan. You have already provided. You already have the solution. We ask You to calm our hearts. Help us to be anxious for nothing. Forgive us for doubting You, for worrying, and for trying so hard to fix everything on our own. Help us to trust You more, help our unbelief. We choose to recognize and to believe that You can accomplish far more and do far greater than we can even ask or think. We thank You in advance for Your answer, for Your provision. Thank You for the abundance of blessing and goodness You have already stored up. We trust You this day and are so grateful for Your Power, for joy, and for Your love. Thank You for teaching us to be content in all circumstances. We love You, Lord, and we are leaning on You. In Jesus name we pray. Amen.

Graduation Saturday had come, and my little cousin Shak was to graduate Summa Cum Laude from Southern Polytechnic University. This was incredible for my young little cousin. I admired anyone that excelled in the university or college setting. I had to study my toosh off to get a "B" and study overtime to get an "A". Although, undergrad and graduate school were quite a challenge for me, but thanks be to God that all things are possible if you believe, and I was given the awesome privilege of completing what I started when it came to my college tenures.

After Shak's graduation, the family returned to my home, and we were able to celebrate Shak's graduation and have an intimate small party with some pictures, pizza, and Vita Malt, which is the family's favorite calorie loaded beverage.

Grandma, Auntie Trudy, graduate Shaka and Shaady.

7
Transformation Starts In The Mind And Heart

It was my first Sunday being home, and I already had my mind made up that I was going to the gathering at "The Corner". I said to myself I will ease back into my normal routine, right! Not so at all. Mi Familia had decided for me, that I needed to rest and slowly get back into the swing of things because I had the trachea and had to walk around with the suction machine and supplies needed to use if I had an emergency and needed suctioning. Mother decided she was not going to the church gathering, so I had no way of getting there. Nevertheless, I had my mind made up that I was going to the gathering, even if I had to walk to get there.

I got dressed, told Mother I was leaving, and left the house. I started out walking towards the church. I walked up to the gas station that was half of a mile from home, where I saw three teenagers in a car and was led to ask them if they wanted to make a quick twenty dollars. The driver looked at me and said, "What do I have to do?" I quickly responded that I needed a ride about twelve miles from where we were. He agreed, and I hopped in and got to the gathering - safely, might I add.

When I got to church, I was able to attend Sunday school. After Sunday school was finished, we transitioned to the worship service. I was able to worship King Jesus in spirit and in truth. It was an awesome experience for me. The thoughts began to flow back to the last time I was there and how a couple of months can surely seem like forever and how things could change at the drop of a dime and we must prepare ourselves for the inevitable, yes, whatever the inevitable may be.

I had the tracheostomy tube in my neck, so I decided to sit in the back of the sanctuary just in case I had to cough and needed to head to the bathroom quickly, so I wouldn't be disturbing anyone too much. The preached word was good. The Word of God always does what it is supposed to do. It washes our minds, hearts, and souls, and every spirit present that day truly celebrated every second of it.

When church was over, my Under-Shepherd, Pastor Brown, gave me a ride home. During the ride

Transformation Starts In The Mind And Heart

home, he began to explain to me that my family cared for me, and he completely understood why they wanted me to take a break. I listened and empathized for a quick second before I gently responded saying, "Pastor, if I am going to go to an outpatient therapy for eight hours a day, five days a week, then truly and most assuredly I can come to the worship service for two hours, one day each week." He looked at me and said, "You are right, Reverend Gumbs, I never thought about it like that," and that was the end of that conversation. When I got home, I settled in and watched some television. About an hour and a half later, Mi Familia came over after attending services by Big Bro.

Remember, I mentioned earlier how the medication I was taking called Prednisone had my hormones flaring. I will now share a special moment I had which I'm not proud to share; however, I want to share my good moments and my not-so-good moments that came with my date with destiny, knowing that all these things have worked together for my good. I believe I was already a little irritated from Mi Familia's decision to not take me to church. When my family came over after church, we all were watching TV when Wandita got up and went over to where my mail is kept at the end of the counter. I really felt insulted that she had not asked me to go through my mail, and yes, I did forget she was the one doing it for the last eight weeks, so I said to her, "Ummm, can I help you look for anything?"

She looked at me and said, "What do you mean?" I said, "Well, you are going through my mail. Is there anything I can help you look for?" She looked at me and said, "If you only knew." Big Bro witnessed what was happening and looked at me and said, "What is going on with you, Kenza? Why are you behaving like that?" I replied, "What do you mean? I know I am sick and recovering, but I still would like to know what's going on in my house." He said, "Kenza, you are focusing on the wrong thing, and I am not going to have you talk to my wife like that, so we are leaving."

They immediately left my home; nevertheless, Grandma, Auntie, Shaady, Shaka, and Mother were still there. They were all uncomfortably quiet and continued watching TV, trying not to say anything that would have escalated the already tense situation. It took me two hours to calm down. After I calmed down, I started to feel terrible about my interactions with Big Bro and Wandita. These were the same people who were with me from the day of my accident to now. They handled all my affairs when I was hospitalized.

They were scheduled to take a cruise the week of my accident and they cancelled it to be at my side. I made up my mind that I had to call them and apologize to them for my outburst. I gave family my love and my goodnights and went upstairs to bed. That night, I climbed into bed with feelings of disappointment. I asked the Lord to forgive me for being a meanie and to help me control these raging hormones. I began to read, and I do not remember anything else until my alarm went off the next day.

    I was disappointed in my behavior and could not wait to call Big Bro and Wandita and apologize for being a complete special one. It is in moments like these I depend on our merciful Father, who looks beyond our faults and sees our needs. Yes, my behavior deserved not being looked out for by Big Bro and Wandita, but thanks be to God who made their hearts turn towards me with compassion, and they looked beyond my faults and saw my needs. Thanks be to our merciful God.

    Getting home was quite an adjustment for me. I was never bothered with my upstairs and downstairs home for the ten years I had lived in it. For the first time since I have lived there, I felt like I was now in for a challenge. But I came up with a plan, which was to take what I needed from the second floor down to the first floor each day, so I did not have to go back and forth. I was home for about a week or so prior to starting outpatient rehab. Boy, oh boy, I never thought in a million years I would be so tired walking up and down the stairs of my home, but I persevered. Not being able to drive myself around, I became dependent on Mother to drive me to the grocery store and pretty much every place I needed to go, and she lovingly did so.

This reality was quite frustrating, but I hung in there. I told myself I can do all things through Christ who strengthens me (Philippians 4:13). I made up in my mind that this too shall pass and, readers, it did pass. One afternoon while getting my mail, I was able to share the story of my accident with one of my neighbors who lived directly across the street from me. He listened in great shock and was happy that I was on my way to recovery. He then shared my story with some of the other neighbors on our street, who did not hesitate to stop by the next day to share their warm wishes and offer their support as well. It was really an incredible and encouraging experience to have my neighbors stop by and show concern and support.

In front of my home was the designated pickup location where some of the middle schoolers hung out and waited for their school bus in the mornings, but that changed after my neighbors learned that I was in recovering mode and needed peace and quiet. They shared with me on that visit that they always said I was thoughtful to have the neighborhood kids wait on my porch for their bus since middle schoolers could be extremely loud at

Transformation Starts In The Mind And Heart

times. Before the accident, this was never a problem for me since most of the time I was never home.

Now that I was home, I regained access to my cellphone. There was some sort of glitch that made me lose all my contact numbers. So, I did what anybody else would have done, I emailed and Facebooked my friends and colleagues and shared with them my accident story and the loss of my contact numbers. My remarkable colleagues and friends came by my home to visit me.

One colleague was very transparent and said to me that she had no idea what she would find when she came to see me and was surprised that I looked quite normal. That alone made her quite relieved, noting the miracle she was witnessing, where her colleague was struck by a train while in her car and came out looking the way I did. I told her it was God who gets all the credit for preserving me. I am reminded of the story of Joseph found in Genesis 37, where God preserved his life. Joseph's brothers were so jealous and hated him so much they sold him into slavery and out of their lives. This spirit is so dangerous that it will make one feel that the wrong being done is right and tries to justify the evil done.

But God preserved his life in the pit, He preserved him in Egypt, and He preserved him from the temptation of Potiphar's wife. Potiphar believed his wife's story of "rape" over Joseph's innocence, and he was sent to prison. Even in prison God preserved his life.

It was in Joseph's prison sentence that God made a way for him to interpret Pharaoh's dream. His accurate interpretation promoted him to one of the highest positions in Egypt. What was meant for evil God turned around for Joseph's good....and He will do the same for us all. God is in control. He is working out His plan. This can be difficult to believe, especially when life seems to be out of control. Yet the God who guided Joseph's destiny is the one who is guiding our destinies. This truth and reality is worth relearning as many times as it takes for our minds to be transformed into this powerful reality of existence!

8
All Things Work Together For Good

The first outpatient therapy was scheduled on Monday to Friday from 8:00 a.m. to 3:00 p.m., but my, my, my, that was not going to work for us. We spent more than an hour and change in traffic trying to get through a twenty-four mile long journey for 8:00 a.m. So, Mother and I headed straight to the program director's office and got my therapy classes adjusted to begin at 10:00 a.m.

My new schedule was much better and more convenient. Outpatient therapy was like inpatient, except that we were able to sit outside and chit chat with each other when we had breaks and lunch times. I remembered mostly everyone that was at inpatient rehab who were now at outpatient rehab, and we got along even better there having a history of inpatient care together.

Date With Destiny

    The second week of being in my own space, I called my dear lady friend whose ordination I was going to attend when the accident occurred. When I called and shared with her my story, she sounded so sad. I told her that all is well, and it was not her fault that this happening occurred. She came over to see me the very next afternoon and spent some time with me, she was also able to meet my mother. We both have moms who look incredibly fantastic for their age.

    At the end of my second week being home, I ran into a big problem. I was taking multiple medications and never thought twice that I was not drinking as much water as I should. Also, I was not taking any stool softeners…and guess what happened? I ended up having major constipation. Every human being alive knows how uncomfortable that problem really is. But thank You, Jesus, for mothers, especially mine. She was not being celebrated because of Mother's Day that had recently passed, but when I cried long tears as I told her my situation, she gently assisted her big baby daughter in reversing the happenings of severe constipation, borderline impaction. I totally respected her for being there to assist me in my extra special time of need that day and for that I am eternally grateful. Love you, Mother.

    Immediately after that intimate episode we went through together, we went straight to Kroger and purchased some Colace, which is a stool softener, because I was not going to get caught in that predicament again. After we got the medication, we went to therapy. I had settled into the outpatient program. Our lunches were in one big lunch room on the inside or outside, and all the patients were able to socialize. My mom began to form bonds with some of the other moms there. It was a very supportive environment.

It was now time for Cornerstone's Vacation Bible School (VBS) for the year 2015, and it was scheduled for June 22 - 26 from 5 p.m. to 8 p.m. I had been the leader of VBS since 2010. We have had successful VBSs so far, and this year was going to be as great as in the past years. We had a fabulous lesson plan entitled, "Message received, hearing God's call," thanks to Park Avenue Baptist Church and Pastor Lanta, who have partnered with us since 2010. They were gracious by donating their left-over props, books, and whatever else I saw that would be beneficial for the lesson.

Pastor Brown and I went down to get the supplies because I still was not able to drive. When I got there, Pastor Lanta and I played catch-up because she had learned about my accident and was so happy to see me. Yes, as always, I was ever so thankful for their generosity. We took everything back to our church for storing purposes. I was able to take

Date With Destiny

the lesson plan home to review the next day, so I could put together our five-day VBS adventure.

Each year, the Lord allowed special kids to participate in our VBS, who were extremely blessed by the lessons taught, and we were hoping that this year would be the same. It would be quite interesting this year for sure. The fact that I was in recovery mode, having therapy sessions, with the tracheostomy, and still not being able to drive, made it quite interesting; nevertheless, it all worked together. On the days leading up to VBS, we were able to sign up ten kids, and for that we were thankful.

The upcoming week was going to be quite busy for me. I had to be quite strategic, making sure I emailed the lesson plan to the group for the upcoming day from the night before. This enabled them to know ahead of time what we were going to do. My scheduled therapy sessions for Monday went as planned. My therapist knew of my ear nose and throat appointment, thus my sessions ended early, so I was able to head down to Buckhead, where the office is located.

My doctor's visit was great up until the point I learned that I was having a buildup of extra tissue around my trachea opening and had to have surgery to remove the tissue being built up. I was not happy about that at all, because this would be the third surgery I would be undertaking. My doctor was not sure of the exact date but shared with me that it would be happening soon. Hearing this news was not grand at all, so I had to ask Jehovah Elohim for strength, which He promised to give to us if we asked, so I asked and received strength in abundance. His strength empowered me to be ready for the VBS starting later that afternoon.

The first day of VBS went well. The kids took everything in with laughs, games, shouts, and great harmony. My team was great as well. I believed my part was performed well despite my apparent limitations. I did not have to scream or yell. Shaady was my designated driver. The second day of therapy and VBS went well as planned. On the third day of therapy, I learned from my ear nose and throat staff that the date of my scheduled surgery was going to be on the fourteenth of July at 10:00am. I placed the date in my calendar so that I could remember.

The next day, my physical therapist and I were talking, and I was moved to ask her about my inability to lay down flat. She seemed surprised to learn of the happenings and began to ask a series of questions and was able to share with me that it appears that I had some crystals moved from my inner ear canal on impact from my accident that was called "otoconia", which is known as Benign Paroxysmal Positional Vertigo or BPPV. She shared that it's the most common cause of vertigo and is also the most common vestibular (inner ear) disorder. BPPV occurs when tiny calcium crystals are displaced from either one or both otolith organs of the inner ear and fall into one of the semicircular canals, disrupting the flow of the fluid of that canal.

The immediate next question I had for her was how were we going to fix this issue? She said through some repositioning maneuvers which incorporate a specific series of head and body movements designed to move the displaced otoconia's out of the involved or affected semicircular canal. This series of movements is typically completed in a short period of time, though repetition of the series can sometimes be required. There are several types of repositioning maneuvers, which are specific to the semicircular canal that is involved. There are some exercises that could be done to get them to roll back in place.

The next day we were at it. I had to lie flat while she performed the maneuvers with my head which kept me still in a certain position over time. It was a dramatic scene. I cried long tears because I felt sick to my stomach. I started to sweat profusely, and I was quite anxious at times and was very loud, but she was able to work with me and maneuvered me into those needed positions to move the displaced crystals back to where they should be.

I was able to get relief about forty-five minutes later. I was finally able to lie flat without my head spinning out of control. I was so happy. Who would have ever thought that you would have crystals in your ear canal that control your balance like that? All I could say after learning this truth was "Wow." Psalm 139:13-14 says, *"For You formed my inward parts; You wove me in my mother's womb. I will give thanks to You, for I am fearfully and wonderfully made; Wonderful are Your works, and my soul knows it very well."*

There are amazing capabilities of the human body God has created. Our bodies are made up of billions of cells and countless parts that can only be adequately explained by a loving and wise Creator and Designer. He has created us with such originality, wisdom, power, and love, and the only proper response is to honor Him and glorify His name. As this Psalm notes, *"Among the gods, there is none like You, O Lord, nor are there any works like Your works. All nations whom You have made shall come and worship before You, O Lord, and shall glorify Your name. For You are great and do wondrous things; You alone are God"* Psalm 86:8-10 (NKJV).

That night was the first night since my "date" I was able to lie flat in my bed. Here I was thinking the trachea was the cause of me not being able to lie flat, and the reality of this happening was caused by the "otoconia". This reality reminds me that we who are Gods people, must be intentional to gather all the necessary facts needed before we come to conclusion/s on a matter/s in our lives. Glory to God.

My scheduled therapies went as planned the remainder of the week. VBS went as planned also and on the last day of VBS, we had a graduation party, presented certificates, took lots of pictures, and were able to share some sweet goodies. God did it again like He did before. He is faithful to all His people indeed.

Reflecting on the awesome week we had last week, now in the middle of our trip to therapy sessions on Monday morning, the car's air conditioning unit went out. When least expected, rain comes, and then it pours. It was hot and quite uncomfortable, having been at the end of June going into July in Georgia. The last thing that was needed was another unexpected expense. Big Bro took it upon himself to call the dealer where the car was purchased and explained the car's condition and my health situation.

They asked us to bring the car in and we did. They called us later that day letting us know the car was ready. The AC stayed cool for one day and was out again. Thank God I knew of a mechanic close by and decided to take it to him. The issues were resolved in two days and at a great price, might I mention. A big shout out to an awesome mechanic name Justin at Justin E Auto Repair, where his mantra is "Auto repairs that work". Thank you for your skills that you use to be a blessing to us and our vehicles, in our time of need. Forever grateful. With the air conditioner working, the heavy heat burden was lifted, so we were able get to and from therapy sessions comfortably.

After having the start of the week challenged with car repairs, I had to get my mind and heart in a restful place because I was to have surgery in a couple of days. The surgery day was now upon me. Surgery under anesthesia always requires one to have nothing by mouth after midnight. The day of surgery is always hard, but I had to do what was required of me. I was scheduled to be there for 10:00 a.m. I got there around 9:35 a.m. I signed in and took a seat in the waiting room until my name was called.

I was led into the operating room where I was given my operating room clothing and escorted to the operating bed and waited for about two minutes. The anesthesiologist was extremely friendly and made me feel comfortable and relaxed. I am always so appreciative of caregivers that are awesome. I have realized that in any field one is called to serve, there is grace upon you that makes what you are called to do easy and makes the one being served comfortable. I believe that is why we must do what we have been called to do, with no exceptions whatsoever. All of us were created for a specified purpose, and we must ask for direction from

Heavenly Father so we can be fulfilled. I am not saying that there will be no challenging days; however, He will lead you and direct you in all your endeavors, where King Jesus will be glorified through you.

In no time I was in "lala" land. When I opened my eyes again, I was in the recovery room. I was not in any pain but was extremely cold. When the nurse asked me if I needed anything, I told her a blanket. She was kind enough to bring me a nice warm one. I hung in there for about twenty to thirty more minutes. My nurse came back to check on me and told me, she was ready when I was. I got up, got myself together, thanked them, and headed home. Once home, I was able to eat, relax, and get myself together for therapy the next day. I was quite satisfied with the outcome of my surgery. No pain at all and for that I was thankful.

The next morning, I was ready to go to therapy. When I didn't hear Mother coming downstairs as she normally did, I called out to her. She said, "I am not feeling well." I asked, "What do you mean, Mother?" She replied, "My head is hurting me." I wished she had me told this earlier, so I could jump to plan B a bit sooner, so I was probably going to be late for therapy. I called a dear friend of mine who was also home from work recovering from an illness but who could drive, so I asked her to give me a ride to therapy. She agreed and came for me and

All Things Work Together For Good

was able to take me to and from therapy. There will always be a ram in the bush for ABBA's children. He truly takes good care of His chosen.

9
Mercy Always Triumphs Over Judgment

While at therapy, a colleague turned friend, who originally is from Georgia, took a traveling assignment down in St. Thomas and was back visiting her family. She asked about Mother, and I told her she was home today because she wasn't feeling well. She asked for the address and said she would stop by and check up on her. I thought it was quite awesome that she was stopping by to say hello to Mother and me. So much had happened since we last met. She met a good man and they were contemplating marriage. I was ecstatic and happy for her.

When I got home, she was upstairs with Mother who was still lying down because she still wasn't feeling any better. My friend asked for my blood pressure cuff and stethoscope, so she could check my mother's blood pressure because she was also a Registered Nurse. Mother's blood pressure was extremely high, scary high to be exact. I now understood what was happening with Mother.

The plan was to continue monitoring her blood pressure through the night and the next day, and if it remained high we would put a call in to Dr. Wanda for the next steps. My friend's visit was a blessing in disguise. Mother was made aware that she had high blood pressure and was able to get the needed medication at no cost to take care of her immediate physiological need. Mother was also being blessed in her sacrifice for her daughter. God is so awesome in ALL His doings! What a Mighty God He is.

The next day came quickly, it was another day for therapy. Therapy went as planned. When I finally got home as I normally did, I went to grab the mail. Going through the countless junk mail, I noticed I had received a letter from my job. Wondering what it was, I opened it as soon as I got inside. Lo and behold, it was a separation notice, dating back to the 10th of July. Here I was with a separation notice with no given reason or explanation as to the making of their decision. This news was extremely heart- breaking for me. I cried like a baby first, got myself together, then called Big Bro and shared the information I had just received.

He calmly said to me, "Kenza, it is going to

be ok." I said to him, "Big Bro, did you hear what I said?" He replied, "I did hear you, Kenza, and like I said before, it is going to be ok." I sincerely anticipate being seasoned with grace to the point of when I get bad news, I am not freaking out but will handle bad news like my Big Bro always does. It is the epitome of trust in motion. Believing what God says above all else. Despite what the obstacle in front of you is telling you, standing on the promises of God with complete trust in God, in the midst of, throughout, and always with confidence.

This resolve state of mind and heart is profound because one does not crumble, do not get fearful or do not have one's feathers ruffled when the Goliath size obstacles are in front of you, but one can stand with confidence, knowing if God is for us, who can be against us? The universal response to this question is no one, no circumstance, no situation, or no lie from the enemy can or will separate us from the love of God. This knowledge gives you a humble and righteous boldness for sure.

The next day, on our way home from therapy I was able to convince Mother, who was feeling much better, to stop at the Burlington coat factory close by. Of course, when you go there and find an outfit that is nice and inexpensive, you get it. I was able to bless Mother and myself because we both had challenging days prior and did not mind looking fabulous.

Buying a new outfit was therapy for me at the time. Unknown to me, of course, Big Bro was paying attention to my spending trends online and called the next day and asked me why I was spending money in places like Burlington, especially at the time with no flowing income.

My response was, "What had happened was, Big Bro, I asked Mother to stop there for a little and I found some cheap pieces and got them." Anytime someone begins an explanation with "What had happened was...." look out.

He then said, "Kenza, why are you spending money on things that are wants and not needs?" My immediate response was, "Hey Big Bro, if money is in the account, and I see something I want, I will get it". He kept quiet and said, "Ok, Kenza, since you feel like that, I will not put any more money into your account then." Not believing him, I smirked and said, "Hey Big Bro, just know that the same God who raised you up to put money in my account will raise someone else up to put money in there if you stop." His quiet response was, "Oh yeah, you feel that way, alright so I will not put anything else in there then." I smirked again and said, "Alright then, will talk to you later."

After having this tough conversation with him, I sat on my couch for about five minutes, got my emotions in check, and prayed silently, asking

ABBA for mercy indeed. I had just allowed my emotions to cut off a source of funding to me which I needed. Sometimes we just let our emotions take us too far, but thank God for mercy from a loving ABBA Father who looks beyond our faults and sees our need. As I stayed put for about five more minutes waiting for an answer, my spirit and mind remembered the words of the song that says, *"When peace like a river attendeth my way, when sorrow like sea billows roll, whatever my lot, thou hath taught me to say, it is well, it is well, with my soul."* Those words brought a peace that I so needed, and I was truly convinced and comforted that all will be well.

Later that day Twinny and I spoke, and I shared with her all the happenings of my day. With her Human Resources background, she shared with me that I should go to the Department of Labor and apply for unemployment and, believe it or not, I was not opposed to it. I came to a moment in my existence where I accepted and allowed help to come to me from whatever resource was out there to help me, including the government.

I Googled where my local Department of Labor office was located and went there with my separation notice and all the other supporting documents that were needed. I waited for about three hours, then I was called into the office with one of the case workers who asked me a slew of questions.

Date With Destiny

When it was all said and done, I got approved for unemployment in the amount of $330.00 a week for thirteen weeks. I gave the approval for them to take out federal and state taxes, which left me with $290.00 per week.

They sent me to another local office to see if I was eligible for any other assistance and was approved for the Supplemental Nutrition Assistance Program or SNAP in the amount of $180.00 a month; to my surprise my SNAP card came two days later. I was very impressed with it, it was like a debit card, where you must put a pin number for it to work. My unemployment monies came directly to my bank account. I was surely relieved that food was not going to be a struggle for my mom and myself, although it was not a problem up to this point. My beloved brother and sister were able to be a blessing in major ways, helping me with all my bills.

I was certainly existing in a place that I had never been before and had no idea this was going to happen all at once. So that Sunday night before I went to bed, I fell on my knees and prayed to the Lord, saying, "Daddy, I have no money to pay my mortgage. You gave me this house ten years ago, and if it is Your will that I lose it, let it be, but if it is not Your will, tell me what to do, so I can hold on to it." Nothing came to my spirit or my mind at that prayer request time. Shortly after that, I peacefully went in my bed and drifted off to sleep soon thereafter.

The next morning while having breakfast, the Lord spoke to my spirit and instructed me to call my mortgage company and ask them what programs they have for people like me, who had a serious accident, lost a job, and was in recovery full time. I was excited that the Lord answered my prayer. I picked up the phone and called Twinny and said, "Girl, the Lord told me to call the bank and ask them what programs they have for clients like me." Her reply was, "Girl, we called the bank already and they said they have nothing for you." A righteous boldness came into my spirit and I said to her, "Did the Lord tell you all to call the bank?" She said, "No, the Lord didn't tell us to call." I immediately said, "Sister, the Lord told me to call and I am going to do what He tells me to do." Smartly she said, "Well, call the bank then, Kenza." I said to her, "Oh yes, I will do that and do it right now." We gave each other our tatas.

I immediately called the bank, introduced myself, told the female representative my loan number, and shared with her what occurred in my life. The representative was very empathetic and very compassionate towards me saying, "Ms. Gumbs, we are so sorry to hear what has happened to you, and yes, we do have programs for clients just like you. Is your email still the same?" To which I replied yes.

She then continued, "Okay, we will send the application to your email that you must fill out, making sure it is filled out in its entirety, and send it back to us with your unemployment papers, including your separation papers, and we will let you know in thirty days what you qualify for here at the bank." When the email with the application came through, I took my time filling out the only thirty-two-page application, attached my separation papers, proof of my SNAP assistance, and my unemployment papers, and sent it to them as requested.

The next day at therapy the recreational as well as physical therapy group I was assigned to took a group of us to the bowling alley and an ice cream parlor to assess our brains in spending accountability. I was super excited because I enjoyed bowling before "my date" and I was still interested in bowling. The other exercise I was not too sure what it was all about. I was leading the group participants so far with the most pins down; however, a few bad balls caused me to lose by one pin.

The competitive side of me surfaced that day. I enjoy competing and, might I add, I also enjoy winning. Then we went to the ice cream parlor. My therapist asked questions concerning spending accountability. Questions like: If you have twenty dollars, how much can you spend so that everyone can get ice cream? There was no trick to it, we just had to get the cheapest ice cream. The lesson behind the encounter was received, and I summed it up to be an awesome outing for all of us.

10
Weeping May Endure For The Night BUT Joy Is Coming

Two weeks had passed, not the thirty days the representative at the bank had said. I got the call from the bank that I was anticipating. When I answered the phone, they politely asked how I was doing today. I replied, "Well, thank you, and you?" The representative said, "Wonderful," then went on to say, "we got great news for you today, Ms. Gumbs. You qualify for the unemployment program here with us, and your new mortgage will be one hundred and eighty-eight dollars and forty-eight cents ($188.48) for twelve months." I screamed out with joy to learn about this miracle that was happening, of course giving all the praise to ABBA.

Right then and there my faith went to another level. I finally understood that if I hold my peace, King Jesus will fight my battle for me. Here I was in the midst of a season where it seemed like all hope was lost, but Jesus came through for me surely, having my most important needs being taken care of, in a way I did not even know existed.

These moments brought me to a solid resolution that is recorded in the book of Romans 8:28 (NKJV) which says, *"All things work together for the good to them that love God and to those who are called according to His purpose."* Yes, I know some of you may be wondering how my accident was purposed by God. And the truth is God did not cause this to happen, but He allowed it to happen. His grace did abound towards me, and through it all, I am able to love, honor, and trust Him despite the experiences that were before me, as hard as they were. I kept my faith in Him, knowing and trusting in Him alone and that His plans during these tough times were good and will always be good. Now to look back and see how all these moments came together in the perfect order, I am completely in awe.

Up next was another appointment with my ear nose and throat doctor. This time it was great to see one of my acquaintances from both inpatient and outpatient rehab in the office waiting area. We played catch -up and I found out she was able to go back to work and was quite happy. When she asked me, "Are you back to work yet?" I replied, "No, not yet." I still did not take the Neuro-psych test. She said, "Oh yeah, I remember that zoo of a test." We both laughed because we both understood what the test determined.

When the time came to separate, she wished me the best on the test, we embraced each other, and I shared my happiness for her in the season of going back to work after such a challenge. It's just amazing how God places you in someone's life and them in yours, so support can be mutual and beneficial. I am eternally grateful for all whom I have met and for all who have met me. May we at designated times and in many ways be each other's strength.

At therapy there was a recreation therapist who was the music minister for Cornerstone Church in the past and was told by one of the Pastors that knew I was there, to look out for me. Think it not strange he took it upon himself to look for me and ministered to me through music and song, which he is so anointed to do. One day therapy arranged for two of my tracheostomy patient buddies and myself to all be in the same room, listening to music together, and it was quite a hilarious moment. Here we were loving music, and neither of us was able to sing because of the tubes in our neck. Looking back, I can now laugh at these moments with a joyful heart.

Date With Destiny

As the needed improvements in my short-term memory came to pass, my therapy sessions decreased from five days a week to three days a week. It was improving slower than I wanted it to, but I gave God thanks for the improvements as slowly as they came. On this morning while I was having breakfast, the thought came to me that I should reach out to an attorney and get a free consultation. I called Big Bro and shared with him my intention of calling an attorney to see if I had a case. He said, "If you want to do that go ahead. Just remember that you were the one at fault in this case and the odds are against you, but if you want to call, go ahead." I contemplated what he said and decided to call them anyway.

I did some research and found an attorney in the city of Atlanta who sent someone out to my home to get an account of my story. I was asked to retrieve a police report from the police station for my accident. I was able to get to the Court House and retrieve my report for five dollars. When I got home and read it over and saw the drawings of my accident, I was moved with tears. It is in moments like these that you realize you cannot take anything for granted, at all. I was able to scan it to the attorney with hopes that he would take my case. After about a week he said he would take the case although it was quite a challenge and he would do his best. About six weeks later, he called and shared with me that after a few consultations with other attorneys, he decided that he would not be able to represent me.

I was disappointed. I was in no state to work since my accident, was still in outpatient rehab, had lost my job and livelihood, and this attorney was telling me I had no case. This news was a complete letdown. This brought me to a place of emotional pain that I had never experienced before. Life at times can be so disappointing. That night I got into my bed and cried for hours. I cried myself to sleep. When I awoke the next morning and after my devotion, I said to Heavenly Daddy, "Ok, so what now, Father? I know you make no mistakes; help me to accept the attorney's decision, help me to be strong and keep moving." I was hurt, but I had to trust that this is all going to work out for my good.

Let me pause here again to encourage those who may be disappointed, whether it's from a failed relationship, a failed job interview, or loss of a promotion you thought you had coming. Just remember, God still cares and loves you. Sometimes God answers us by saying, "No, not yet." In Philippians 4: 6-7 it says, "Be anxious for nothing, but in everything, by prayer and supplication, with thanksgiving, let your requests be made known to God. And the peace of God, which surpasses all understanding, will guard your hearts and your minds through Christ Jesus."

You can and will overcome every disappointment, when you believe in God's plan. He is a miracle worker. He can and will part waters, heal the sick, raise the dead. He can do everything beyond our wisdom and comprehension. *"For My thoughts are not your thoughts, nor are your ways My ways,' says the Lord. For as the heavens are higher than the earth, so are My ways higher than your ways, and My thoughts than your thoughts." Isaiah 55:8-9 (NKJV)*

Surely, He can and will help you in your situation. Believe that God has the situation under control. Your next step in overcoming disappointment is to grieve your loss. Yes, it's okay to feel sad that things did not go the way you had planned. God is near those who are of a broken heart. *"The Lord is near to the brokenhearted and saves the crushed in spirit." Psalm 34:18.* Next you need to turn the situation over to God by praying. Then listen and wait for his next instructions. Wait no matter how long the desire is taking.

Mighty things happen when we pray. It opens the eyes and ears of God: *1 Peter 3:12 -"For the eyes of the Lord are on the righteous and his ears are attentive to their prayer, but the face of the Lord is against those who do evil."* Sometimes God makes things happen immediately, but sometimes He makes us wait. This is between you and God. He will urge you when the time is right. *"Wait patiently for the Lord. Be brave and courageous. Yes, wait patiently for the Lord."* - Psalms 27:14.

Here is a prayer for you, if and when life does not go your way and you are feeling disappointed:

Dear Heavenly Father, Oh how my heart aches as I bow before you. I thought I knew what was best for me, But I was wrong. My plans did not happen the way I wanted. Now I feel so disappointed. I'm disappointed with the outcome, in people, and my life. Negative thoughts are overtaking my mind; I'm feeling overwhelmed, dear Lord. I need Your help. Have mercy on me. I need strength to trust in You and to replace the negative thoughts. Joy has left my heart; I need to be filled as only You can fill me. May praise return to my lips. For You never disappoint. In the name of Jesus, Amen.

In the midst of all these happenings, I had to go to see my ear nose and throat doctor again for another assessment of this special airway of mine. And as in my prior three visits, the tracheostomy in my neck was still not able to be removed. My doctor said I still had some swelling in my nasopharyngeal area, and he wanted to leave it in just a while longer to be sure. I begged him not to increase the Prednisone doses because it was making me so emotional and highly irritated, short tempered, and whatever else mood that was going haywire due to the steroids. He decided to discontinue the steroids, and I was so happy for that, although the trachea was going to be there for a little while longer.

Outpatient therapy continued Mondays, Wednesdays and Fridays now, and I was so happy for the travel break. I thought that I was doing quite well. The time finally came for me to take this Neuro-psych test that would show that I am able to return to work and to continue my life, just like it was before. I was excited. After taking the test I had to wait a week or so to get the results. In between my test and getting the results, Twinny came up to spend our birthday together. We had a peaceful birthday as six months earlier, I was in the fight of my life, but thanks be to God I was still here making the water produce waves.

My sister went with me to the long-awaited meeting results. I was not cleared to go back to work. Nevertheless, I was devastated. The recommendation was to continue to attend speech therapy for three more months. Thank the Lord, Twinny was there with me to keep me from being overly upset as I was filled with grief and disappointment. We were able to do sister things together, which allowed me to take my mind off the test results I was not happy to have received.

The next week I decided to apply for disability

after learning I was going to be in therapy for three more months. I said to my Heavenly Father, "If it is Your will that I am no longer able to work, Lord, let it be that I am approved for disability." I never in a million years thought that this was going to be my portion; however, "Your will be done, Lord." I was able to get the needed reports from my doctors that the Disability Office requested, and I waited. Still attending outpatient therapy three times a week, I finally heard from the Office of Disability and was to meet with them downtown for an interview. After asking me question upon question, the Specialist said that I would get their decision in the mail in approximately two weeks.

That Monday morning, I went immediately to my vocational therapist and shared my disability meeting experience with him. We then planned to commit to more memory games to improve my deficits. I was completely determined now to press in and hang in there for two weeks.

At the end of the second week, I got the letter that my claim was denied, the reason being determined that my injury was not being classified as permanent. They determined that my injury was classified as temporary. Oddly enough, though I did not qualify for disability, I was quite happy that they came to the conclusion also that I would recover and so I continued my intense intentional journey to total recovery and to get to the place where I can safely go back to work.

The month of September started out tough and challenging. Learning that I was not able to return to work for three more months and with the possibility of not being able to have this apparatus out of my neck would have been a double whammy. But thanks be to God, that He giveth more grace.

Let me share an intimate part of my life, as if the constipation story was not intimate enough. I was dating someone for a year and a half before my date occurred, and one week after my thirty-seventh birthday, he came to me and said our season had come to an end. I asked him, "When did you come to that conclusion?" He replied, "Last week." I pondered on what I was hearing and gave it some thought. The truth is, he left me three months prior to his verbal announcement. However, thanks be to God, who gives more grace when it is truly needed, I chose not to include him in my story up until this point because I wanted to be extremely transparent regarding the reality of my designated date. My finances were attacked, my health was attacked, my love life was attacked, but I was still standing. Standing on the promises of God, as weak and as vulnerable as I felt.

Although I was extremely hurt and disappointed when this happened, I was able to rebound from this with Abba's help. Looking back at that moment, I am forever thankful God worked this one out for me beyond my wildest dreams. You see, I'm glad that God always knows what's best for us. Marriage vows say that you are to love your spouse for better or worse. This was my "worse," and the person I assumed would be there for me decided he wanted out.

I must add this for you ladies out there who have been disappointed by the one you thought was the one! Fret not yourself, God's got you right where you need to be. Let Him heal your mind, body, and heart, which then brings the refreshing and renewal your soul truly needs. Jehovah Shalom will give us that peace which is beyond our mental capacity, to stand! Every one of ABBA's plans for us is good and not evil. Thus, when He permits one to leave our lives, truly it is for our good. Good is good on any given day of the week. Good will always be good in the coming seasons and beyond.

A prayer for a Godly Spouse:

Dear Lord, Your Word declares that if I delight myself in You, you will give me the desires of my heart (Psalm 37:4). At the beginning of creation, You proclaimed, "It is not good that man should be alone" and so You created Eve to be a suitable partner for Adam. Even today,

Father, desiring a spouse is normal because marriage is honorable (Hebrews 13:4). In the name of Jesus, I ask that You protect the person You have chosen for me. Because the covenant of marriage is sacred and the bed is undefiled, I ask for a man/woman of God. Please give me a spouse whose love for me is only outmatched by their love for You; a spouse who will uplift and cherish me, a person who will honor me and our marriage vows; a person to whom I will be attracted to physically, emotionally, and spiritually. Keep me from being unequally yoked. Father, please give me the patience to wait on You and not attach myself to anyone out of desperation. I will not settle for a relationship that is second best. Release me from the baggage of past relationships and prepare me for the person You have chosen for me. Free me from any hindrances to a healthy and godly marriage, Father, be it low self-esteem, past sins, or emotional pain. I place my trust in You rather than my partner. In this period of waiting, I will look to You alone to be my companion and best friend. In Jesus' name I pray. Amen.

11
Waiting On The Lord Is Always Best

Therapy came and went this day, and at 2:00 pm I was with my ear nose and throat doctor. I got to the room, had my assessment, and after what seemed to be like the longest pause, my doctor turned to me and said, "Okay, we will take it out." I was relieved, happy, and excited, all at the same time. I wanted to cry, and I did. This was a significant lesson about times. *"To everything there is a season and a time for every purpose under the heavens."* (Ecclesiastes 3:1).

It was my time of release from this burden. Times and seasons are so important for us, God's people. We must trust His timing for everything. I was so excited to be trachea free, I smiled all the way home. My heart was filled with joy, relief, and peace.

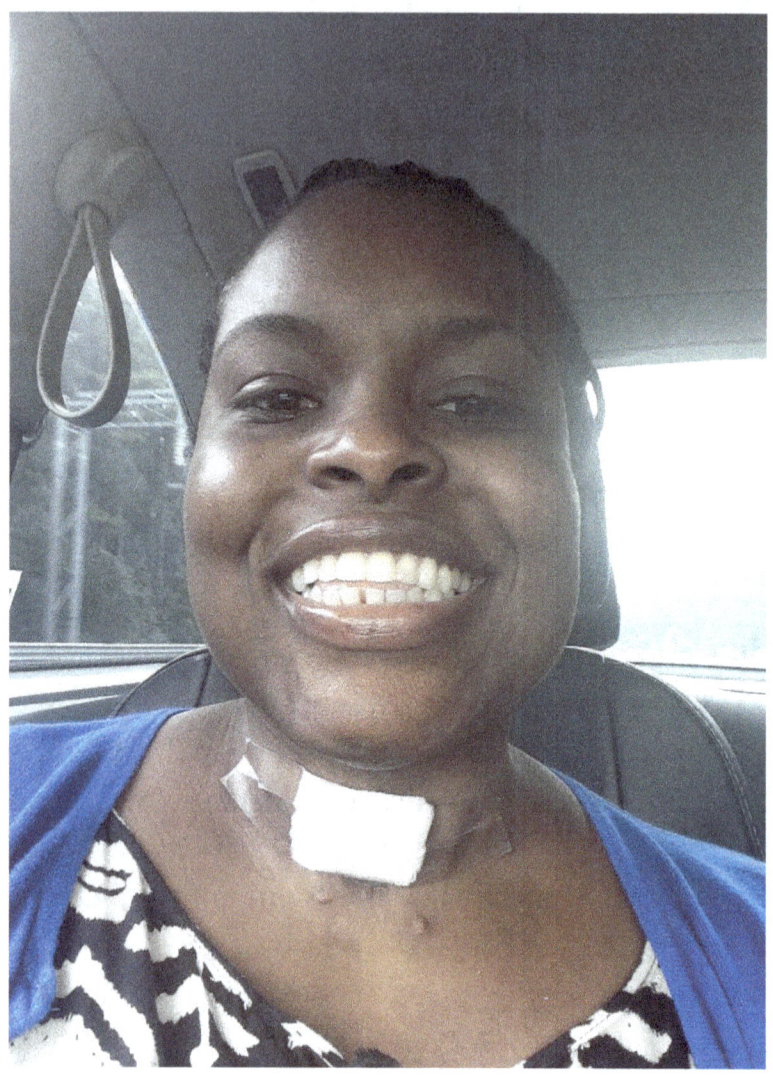

The journey thus far had been extra difficult with the trachea, on top of not being able to drive myself around, which was done so effortlessly before. The next major happening in September was my driving test, which would give me the privilege of driving again. I was extremely happy for this day because it was such a challenge not being independent in this area. I had to depend on the Holy Ghost for peace and patience in this area which He supplied in abundance.

That afternoon after therapy, I went to the instructor's office. He asked a slew of questions including the current transmission of the car I would be driving. When I told him the car I would be driving was manual, he replied, "Then you will have no problem with this test." We walked out to a nice Oldsmobile that was long and much older than I thought it would be. I was at peace, knowing that I will do well through grace. I made sure mirrors were adjusted properly, pulled my seat up to where I was comfortable, ensured the seat belt was on, then started the car.

We headed out on the road, I followed all the instructions given. Maintained the speeding limit on each street that I could see, ensured indicator lights were on in turning positions and coming to a complete stop at stop signs. I felt like I was taking my driving test again, but I persisted and after about forty-five minutes, he said, "You did well, Ms. Gumbs, we can go back to the center now." When we got back to the center, he said, "I will send the typed-up results in and you should be ready to go by tomorrow." I was content at last to be back in the driver's seat of a car.

I was led to go up to the inpatient rehab floor where I was a patient not too long ago. Everyone was quite happy to see me. We hugged, laughed, and caught up on what was happening in my world since I left inpatient therapy. One young lady jokingly said, "Now you are driving again, Kenza. Tell me where and when, and I will make sure not to go on that street." I thought that was extremely funny, and I laughed at her remark. One young lady also jokingly placed her finger up, moving it back and forth, saying, "You loved your little finger when you were here." I laughed at that remark because it was so true. I remember saying no to lots of things. Wow, I could only imagine me back then, but thanks be to God for grace.

There was no therapy the following day, so I jumped in my car and headed over to where the accident occurred. When I got there, I drove over the same train tracks and drove over to the other side of the street where the gas station is located. I got out of my car, walked over to the end of the road, and just looked over to where the accident occurred on the tracks. In my mind and heart, I began to give God glory and praise for His wonderful works towards me. After having my "come to Jesus" moment of reflection, I got in my car and headed home.

God's faithfulness towards me from the beginning of my date with destiny, up through present day, produced a shift in my understanding and brought me to a place of solitude. From my finances, to transportation, to food, to every assistance I received, I finally through all these moments understand that God means what He says and says what He means.

I was asked by Pastor to bring the preached word to the gathering on September 26, 2015. I initially said to myself, I wanted my vocal cords to be much improved before I preached. Multiple thoughts came into my mind, and I had to release the Holy Ghost to go to war for me. I had to make up in my mind, that God allowed this to occur for His glory and not mine. I also asked the Lord for grace. He gives more grace to us, His children. Since the accident and the trachea, my voice was almost hoarse-like and a whisper. I asked God to allow me to embrace and accept my new voice, or my new normal voice, for however long He wanted it to be so.

It was six months in the making, three surgeries later, and I was finally at a place of being at peace with my vocal cords. I enjoyed preaching. I believe with all my heart that preaching is wrapped up in my DNA. I was so thankful I was being allowed to do what I was created for. This moment was so delicate to me that my heart was overwhelmed with joy. My Beloved Bro. Norman sang this awesome worship song during the praise and worship portion of the service named, "There Will Be Victory After

This" by J.J Hairston and Youthful Praise. He turned in my direction, pointed his finger to me and ministered to me in song.

Music ministry under God's anointing is so powerful, I now understand why the enemy always attacks the music ministry first in churches. Judah, which also means "praise," was the most powerful and important tribe out of twelve tribes in Israel. Jesus, our King, (Revelations 5:5) is also known as the Lion of the Tribe of Judah because He prevailed to open the scroll and to loose its seven seals after Apostle John began to weep because no one else was qualified to open the scroll.

The text from the preached Word came from Hebrews chapter 4:1-6, entitled "Enter in Already". The lesson taught on the rest that we who are God's people have in Him, and yet He gives us the choice to enter in this rest or not to enter in. What I love about ABBA Father is that He allows one to choose or not to choose, and He allows one to be or not to be. With all these experiences, I knew beyond the shadow of a doubt that I decided to enter in ABBA's rest, freely and willingly, and was also encouraging my brothers and sisters in Christ to do the same. It was a blessing being a blessing, giving Him all the praise.

My dearest Mother was now able to return home. She assisted me when I needed it the most and for that I was grateful. I am eternally grateful that

Mother and I were able to settle some disagreements that transpired in my earlier years of life. Grace was given to us, and we were able to forgive each other and move on. I finally was able to embrace her with thanksgiving, looking back at those challenging teenage years with hope, knowing that God is a God of second chances.

God worked this one out for me beyond my wildest dreams and for that, He gets all the glory. Sometimes even for Christians, forgiveness is hard because we feel that our reason for holding on to unforgiveness is justified. The Bible says we must forgive, but we say, "God, You do not know what he/she did to me...surely you did not hear what they said about me." Our awesome Father is the creator of forgiveness, and so it belongs to Him and He lavishes us with it every day. Luke 17:3-4 (NKJV) says, *"Pay attention to yourselves! If your brother sins, rebuke him, and if he repents, forgive him, and if he sins against you seven times in the day, and turns to you seven times, saying, 'I repent', you must forgive him."*

God exercises so much patience with us when we are disobedient to what His Word says about forgiveness. We do not forgive but we pretend we are following His Word. Skipping and dancing in church but holding on to unforgiveness against your brother or sister. Holding onto unforgiveness is likened to drinking rat poison but hoping the rat will die. By holding onto the desire to get even, you continually drink the toxic poison of unforgiveness, hoping to get back at the person who hurt you. Unforgiveness is like a boomerang – you can throw it at the person who has hurt you, but it eventually comes back and hits you.

Just as I mentioned earlier about Joseph and how God preserved his life, the story of Joseph also demonstrated the awesome power of forgiveness. You see, even after many years, Joseph was able to forgive his brothers who sold him in slavery and lied to their father. Jesus spoke to this same issue when He answered Peter's question about forgiving someone who repeatedly offends you in Matthew 18: 21-22. *"Then Peter came to Jesus and asked, 'Lord, how many times shall I forgive my brother or sister who sins against me? Up to seven times?' Jesus answered, 'I tell you, not seven times, but seventy times seven."* Mom and I had to each follow God's instruction and forgive each other.

Being now able to drive back and forth to therapy, to church, the grocery store, or wherever I wanted to go, I was able to do it by myself. I took my time on the road, being mostly aware of street signs, especially railroad crossings. I certainly covered myself each day under the blood of Jesus, asking the Holy Spirit to go before me, making all crooked places straight and every rough area smooth. No longer was I taking anything for granted.

Waiting On The Lord Is Always Best

After an encounter of one's date with destiny, one can choose to be angry, annoyed, depressed, or one can choose to be content. I have chosen to be content with my "date" and to be thankful for everything in it and around it. I choose not to be anything other than thankful. I have learned this simple yet profound truth: In everything that unfolds in my life, I choose to give thanks to God because this is what He wants and expects from me. 1 Thessalonians 5:18 (NKJV) says: *"In everything give thanks; for this is the will of God in Christ Jesus for you."*

I persevered all the way through therapy and was discharged December 15, 2015, with the approval to return to work. December 15, 2015, would make it exactly nine months since my accident. Used forty-nine times in Scripture, the number nine symbolizes divine completeness or conveys the meaning of finality. Christ died at the ninth hour of the day to make the way of salvation open to everyone. There are also nine fruits of the spirit. *"But the fruit of the Spirit is love, joy, peace, longsuffering, gentleness, goodness, faith, meekness, temperance: against such there is no law."* (Galatians 5:22)

After my date with destiny, I am a recipient of the nine fruits of the Spirit. Yes, there were times when it got challenging. I felt discouraged and just in a bad state of mind, but through it all, I am eternally grateful that it all happened. I have learned so much about others but most importantly about myself and who I am and who I am not. I do not believe that anything else besides this date would have brought me to this place of complete trust and dependence in our Eternal God.

After being released from therapy, in truth all I wanted to do was to go to Grandma and Grandpa's house and eat some of Grandma's delicious food and receive love from my grandparents. My Grandma is the most inspiring woman I know. I always joke with her in telling her she is leaving a legacy that is very hard to beat. She laughs and then lovingly says, "it is the grace of God, Ken." It is by the grace of God I am here. I so needed to be around them, especially Grandma, so I booked my ticket, and I was in Anguilla the next week for an entire month. While there, I greatly enjoyed my family and friends on the island like never before. My hopes for everyone reading my story is to trust our Savior and Lord even when you do not know what the end will be. Count every experience as a lesson - lessons that lead and guide us into the next season of our existence.

Yes, there are going to be days when there is pondering on what the Lord is up to, where many questions and concerns come to the surface of one's mind. But here is the testimony of someone who has been in an extremely challenging place for a season of time and can now stand boldly and tell you that it is all working together for our good. God, Who loves us more than we will ever know, will cause the love from our family, friends, and even our enemies to be the source of the countless blessings that lead to our full restoration in Him. We are then able to say with a peaceful heart and mind, it was good for me that I was afflicted.

My friends, please remember at the appointed and ordained time, please avoid turning to drugs, money, people, social media, or whatever else is out there. These things may provide a temporary fix or may appear good for a time. I am encouraging you to turn to our loving and eternal Father through His Son Christ Jesus, in whom "all things" consist (Colossians 1:17).

Stand up, stand in Christ alone in the time and season of your "date with destiny" because everything is in His hands! God's bountiful blessings upon you.

References

- Chronos Kairos Christos Literature: Ray Summers: ISBN-13: 9780865545823: Mercer University Press; 09/01/1998

- Diffuse Axonal Brain Injury. Brain Injury Institute. Retrieved from https://www.brain-injuryinstitute.org.

- Kenneth L. Barker. (2002). *Zondervan NIV Study Bible.* Fully rev. ed. Grand Rapids: Zondervan.

- *New International Version.* [Colorado Springs]: Biblical, 2011. Retrieved from http://www.BibleGateway.com. Web. 3 Mar. 2011.

- The English Standard Version Bible: Containing the Old and New Testaments with Apocrypha. Oxford: Oxford UP, 2009. Print.

- *The New King James Version Bible;* 1982 by Thomas Nelson

P.O. Box 453
Powder Springs, Georgia 30127

www.entegritypublishing.com
info@entegritypublishing.com
770.727.6517

www.ingramcontent.com/pod-product-compliance
Lightning Source LLC
Chambersburg PA
CBHW052057070526
44584CB00017B/2227